Holy Faces

26 Reflections

Julie K. Aageson

WIPF & STOCK • Eugene, Oregon

HOLY FACES
26 Reflections

Wipf & Stock
An Imprint of Wipf and Stock Publishers
199 W. 8th Ave., Suite 3
Eugene, OR 97401

www.wipfandstock.com

PAPERBACK ISBN: 979-8-3852-0190-7
HARDCOVER ISBN: 979-8-3852-0191-4
EBOOK ISBN: 979-8-3852-0192-1

VERSION NUMBER 11/21/23

With love and gratitude for siblings who continue to be holy faces in my life: sisters, Marcia K. Wilson and Laurie Taylor VanderWeyst. They are central in the circle of "wise women" whose lives are inherently woven into my own. I also wish to honor and remember my brother, Martin Scott Taylor, whose grievous death I share in the reflection, "Prodigal and Beloved." Last but hardly least, I give thanks for newborn granddaughter, Svea, whose new life and holy face is celebrated in "Unspeakable Joy!" Holy faces, all!

Contents

Cover acknowledgment

“Festival of Lights” copyright 2000 is used with permission from the John August Swanson Trust. I am grateful for the holy face and prolific work of artist John August Swanson. This painting together with many others reflects what it means to “make of yourself a light” and to be a holy face.
(Serigraph, 30.75 x 24) www.JohnAugustSwanson.com

Acknowledgments

I WISH TO ACKNOWLEDGE and thank several people who are included in *Holy Faces* in one way or another. For her ability to capture the essence and the honesty of life together, I am grateful to Louise Erdrich, Minnesota writer extraordinaire, whose quote that begins "Life will break you . . ." from national bestseller *The Painted Drum*[1] helped shape my own writing in *Holy Faces*. Erdrich's gift for acknowledging wrenching loss while inviting readers to taste and savor the goodness of life is a life lesson for all of us. She is quoted in the preface and in the reflection "Breathe with Me," and is among the women referred to in the closing reflection, "Wise Women." I also wish to thank Dr. Brian K. Blount, whose life and work is highlighted in "Blood in the Streets, Devastation in the Land." This reflection was prompted by a letter Blount wrote to alumni of Union Presbyterian Seminary in September 2020. He is the recently retired former president and professor of New Testament at Union Presbyterian Seminary in Richmond and Charlotte, Virginia. I am indebted to Dr. Blount for his prophetic voice, his courage, and his hope.

The ubiquitous presence in life and in death of Archbishop Desmond Tutu is highlighted in the reflection bearing his name. Thank you to Elizabeth Merrill Hoster for her lovely tribute to Tutu. Currently she is priest in charge at St. Luke's Episcopal Church in Granville, Ohio. Helen Jane Rommereim lives in a small house on the grounds of her daughter's farm in northwest Montana. At

1. See Erdrich, *Painted Drum*, 274.

age ninety-eight, she continues to meet regularly with a spiritual formation group for women even as she shares extraordinary hospitality around her own table and in the homes of her children and others.

I also am indebted to Parker J. Palmer and Mary Oliver, two prolific poets and writers whose work enriches the lives of so many American readers. Palmer, a Quaker, is the founder and senior partner emeritus of the Center for Courage and Renewal. He has written numerous books, several of them best-selling and award-winning titles. Among my favorites is *Let Your Life Speak: Listening for the Voice of Vocation.* A lyric writer of both poetry and prose, Oliver won numerous awards, including the National Book Award and a Pulitzer Prize. Her luminous and sometimes numinous writing is often about nature and the "intersection between the human and the natural world" in which she found great peace. She died in 2019.

Kyler Vogt is director of next-generational ministry at St. Andrew Lutheran Church in Beaverton, Oregon. His interaction with youth and young adults is highlighted in "Sentient Dolphins and Existential Questions." Brian Doyle, former editor and writer for *Portland Magazine* and author of *Mink River*, *Martin Marten*, and *One Long River of Song: Notes on Wonder and the Spiritual and Non-Spiritual Alike*, among others, is another holy face whose uncanny reverence for the natural world and its inhabitants, both animate and inanimate, resonates deeply among his devoted readers, myself included. Doyle died in 2017.

Holy Faces includes many others whose lives have intersected with my own, faces known and unknown, animate and inanimate, named and unnamed, all of them part of the fabric of my life. The last reflection in *Holy Faces* is titled "Wise Women." It describes the impact of the exemplary women with whom I have journeyed over many decades. I am grateful for each of you.

Finally and by no means last, I wish to thank Mexican-Swedish-American John August Swanson, the artist who painted the serigraph, *Festival of Lights*, that graces the cover of *Holy Faces*. It reflects the theme of this book on so many levels. Swanson's deep humanity can be seen in the faces of nearly all his creations. In his description of *Festival of Lights*, he recalls liturgical processions, walking with groups in candlelight as they marched for peace in Central America, and the symbol of candles shining in the dark of night. I chose it because it so captures the holy faces of all who seek light, peace, and nonviolence including the surrounding mountains and forests and all their inhabitants. John August Swanson died in 2021.

Preface

Whether reflecting on images from old family photos, seeing the faces and hearing the voices of ancient or modern-day prophets, or finding solace in untold numbers of holy faces in the natural world (where hummingbirds fly and black bears roam), *Holy Faces* is an eclectic, perhaps quirky collection of essays and meditations. It celebrates joy and beauty and acknowledges sorrow and grief. Perhaps most of all, the reflections share a reverence for things animate and inanimate, an awareness of the mysteries of life, and a longing to know who we are, who and what God is, and what the world is like. In their diversity, each conveys a sense of awe and wonder as they point to something beyond mere observation, a deeper and more profound encounter than may first meet the eye. It is this sense of wonder that evokes the word, holy. It is this understanding of faces that underscores each reflection.

I didn't intend to embrace another writing project but in 2020, just as I was finishing *Finding Home* and preparing to send it off to my publisher, a pandemic came thundering into our lives. It was early spring and we could not yet fathom the implications of a worldwide epidemic, a literal plague (or pestilence in the vocabulary of my English friends) that would stop nearly every country and community in their tracks. We watched because we could *not watch*. The isolation of the pandemic seeped into our lives and no amount of social interaction could assuage our longing for one another's faces. After that long season of isolation and darkness, some of which included faces hidden behind masks, the life-giving reality of being able to see one another had never felt so hallowed, so holy.

The extraordinary voice of Minnesota writer, Louise Erdrich, in her book *The Painted Drum*, reminds us of the truth of life: "Life will break you. Nobody can protect you from that, and living alone won't either, for solitude will also break you with its yearning. You have to love. You have to feel. It is the reason you are here on earth. You are here to risk your heart. You are here to be swallowed up. And when it happens that you are broken, or betrayed, or left, or hurt, or death brushes near, let yourself sit by an apple tree and listen to the apples falling all around you in heaps, wasting their sweetness. Tell yourself you tasted as many as you could."[2]

With Louise Erdrich and many others, I do not wish to ignore the harsh realities of everyday life. We are made to love and to risk and to feel. With Desmond Tutu, I believe we are made for goodness and with John Lewis, we need to "make good trouble." With Mary Oliver and Brian Doyle, I want to see all of creation as sacred, holy—places where God shows up. Without a lot of God-talk, both writers leave no doubt in their stunning writing about the presence of God. Their reverence for nature is itself holy and their passionate love of life and of humanity is authentic. God shows up in the life and work of Brian Doyle in mountains that speak and martens that communicate with humans, in the life of a crow named Moses and a village by the sea. Parker Palmer reminds us to love life fiercely, all of life. With Julian of Norwich, we seek to understand the meanings of creation, incarnation and resurrection, of life and death, of God.

In *Holy Faces,* I write about interaction and relationship, communication spoken and unspoken, the spirit of our shared humanity, our relationship with nature and creatures great and small. I include stories of my family, people whose lives have graced my own paying attention to the joys and sorrows that mark all our lives. I too invite readers to sit under an apple tree—to listen and to taste and experience holiness, the goodness of life. I write about circumstances that are life-giving and people who, in spite of all

2. Erdrich, *Painted Drum*, 274.

the darkness, find light and hope and truth that includes joy in life together. My wish is that readers will find here stories of compassion and generosity, honesty and humility, ways of seeking the sweetness of life among the heaps of fallen apples as prescribed by Louise Erdrich. These are the faces where I see God.

Julie K. Aageson

1

A Motley Crew

THE FACES IN THE old photo taken so long ago are a trip back in time. Now faded and in the sepia hues of photos one hundred years old, the picture is of Ingeborg, my great-great grandmother dutifully and dourly standing off to one side, no smile, no sense whatsoever of pleasure over this freshly minted four-generation gathering, simply matter-of-fact and obligatory. On the right-hand side of the photo stands her daughter, my great-grandmother, Helena, whose face shows a wisp of sober pleasure in spite of—by that time—the deaths of three husbands and the care of many children, her own and those orphaned by the deaths of their own mothers. And in the center of this serious lot is Martha, my maternal grandmother who holds her firstborn child, a boy perhaps six or seven months old. She too is sober but seems quite taken with this little son and perhaps pleased to be the center attraction in the marking of four generations.

The now-worn photo, likely taken at a family gathering on a well-remembered Pacific Northwest island beach, shows lives filled with difficult passages. Ingeborg's journey with her husband and five or six young children, including then-baby Helena, was on a crowded ship; days and weeks were spent at sea packed together like sardines on their way to a new world where they hoped to begin a better life than they'd known in the old country. Family lore doesn't paint Ingeborg kindly; no doubt the challenges of her life had taken a toll. Her daughter, Helena, was a social child, good-natured, and carrying the advantages of having grown up in this country. But Helena's life too was filled with much loss and the weight of all those children, her own and their own, plus the children of two of three husbands whose first wives' premature deaths left them desperately in need of mothers and partners to make their way in life a bit less complicated.

My own grandmother was the first of Helena's tribe but the older stepbrothers and sisters quickly took their place in the menagerie. I can imagine that family life was fraught with complicated relationships and aching losses as well as economic hardship and Martha's sense of responsibility for her younger siblings. This grandmother of mine was seriously studious and her mother never stopped reminding her that her father who'd died while she was still a toddler was a scholar and a pastor and she, Martha, carried his genetic disposition for learning. In a day when women were not encouraged to get a formal education, Martha went on to graduate from high school and a two-year college before being certified as a public school teacher. After the death of Helena's second husband in North Dakota, she returned to the family farm in Minnesota and some years later packed up her gaggle of children, including Martha, to join other family members living on the West Coast. When Martha married my grandfather, a son of Helena's third husband, they were teased mercilessly for being siblings even though they hadn't grown up together. My grandfather had suffered the loss of his mother when he was eleven years old and he too was working to find his own way, now in the Pacific Northwest.

These are my people. My grandfather's formal education ended in the eighth grade. But like my grandmother, he valued education and was a lifelong learner. From my grandparents and my own parents, I absorbed a keen sense of the value of education, spoken and unspoken but clearly a road map to be followed. My grandfather's rolltop desk was front and center in their big Arts and Crafts style home and he became a successful financial advisor and investor. He loved geography and maps and was curious about and interested in people from all walks of life. My grandmother was a public school teacher and after marrying, she continued teaching Sunday School and adult groups for years, all the while instilling her love of learning in her own children.

From this motley crew of Scandinavians and from my own parents whose lives were shaped by family commitments and sometimes conflicting notions of religion and faith, I learned who I was and who I wanted to be. From them—a pious bunch who never failed to begin and end the day with prayer, who never missed Sunday worship and never failed to critique the sermon and the one in the pulpit who preached with a cadence and rhythm so mesmerizing that I still recall its beat and tempo to this day—from these people of mine who chafed over card playing and dancing and looked down on family members who jumped ship to join the Pentecostals or the Baptists, from them I learned in spite of all the warts and inconsistencies that I was loved beyond measure and that the source of that love was a God of grace. Even in our arrogant and never-wavering sense of "having found the truth" of religion and a life of faith, I learned from these quirky and peculiar generations of family a resilient faith and sense of identity. Their faith was intertwined with deep family roots and with a larger understanding of something bigger than family or cultural identity or denominationalism—a creator God, the Holy One, the Jesus in the manger and on the cross, the Christ of the universe.

They taught me perseverance and resilience, discipline and responsibility. I learned from them—in spite of their sometimes rigid notions and hang-ups about bodies and sex, marriage and divorce, alcohol and gambling, and anything else done in excess—to embrace questions, live with uncertainty, and struggle with belief. It helped that my father, new to religion and able to get at the heart of grace without the pious trappings, discovered himself to be the recipient of God's love and taught me that same love. I learned from him and my mother and the generations before them that there is a God and I am not it. Nor am I the center of the universe or the fulcrum around which life spins. And I learned too that I am made in the image of God, that my life is prized and priceless, that I matter to them and to others and most of all to God.

So in spite of dour grandmothers carrying heavy baggage and arrogant ancestors and mental health issues and guilt and shame over alcoholic siblings whose drunken presence would evoke hymn singing by pious sisters, in spite of condemning the Pentecostal relatives to hell and the Baptists to the pit of bad theology or questioning with knowing eyes what was done in order to become pregnant, in spite of divorce and a notion of being "the chosen ones," of rampant judgmentalism and a ubiquitous corner on the truth, I learned from this motley crew the goodness of life. Because somehow among all the inconsistencies and embarrassingly irritating yet human qualities and characteristics, this band of mine somehow found joy and hope and love, the resonance of which has shaped my life. Like few other photos in my collection, this one of my three grandmothers and a favorite uncle evokes for me a visceral sense of the convoluted yet generative, life-giving, and complicated facts of family history. Holy faces to be sure.

REFLECTION

From this motley and perhaps quirky crew of ancestors, I learned who I was and who I wanted to be. From them, I discovered the goodness of life.

- When you look at old family photos, what do you see? Who are some of the holy faces in your ancestry?
- Are there family stories you recall that shaped who you are and what you value? Describe one or two.
- "Their faith was intertwined with deep family roots and with a larger understanding of something bigger than family or cultural identity or denominationalism." Does this resonate for you and/or your family? Why or why not?
- How might that larger understanding shape your life today?

2

Blood in the Streets, Devastation in the Land

ANY THINKING, FEELING ADULT learns quickly that one's childhood view of life—if it's been relatively healthy and trouble-free—is altered dramatically as the complex realities of life begin to surface. When the grief of the world can no longer be held at bay, when we begin to feel the injustices and notice that once dependable foundations can be ripped away, our rose-colored glasses no longer work. The last several years have shown us how quickly the ground beneath our feet can crumble. Living with privilege, good health, and a propensity for optimism has allowed many of us to keep our heads down, our accounts intact, and an ever-fragile sense of security in place. Most of the time, we find balance between despair and hope, active engagement and quiet contemplation. But in daily life, the realities of this twenty-first century are grim reminders that there is indeed blood in the streets and devastation in the land.

On one of those wringing-of-hands days when despair loomed large, a letter arrived from an acquaintance. On the one hand, I had only just been writing about politics gone awry, the frustrations of pandemic life, and the graphic explosion of people living on the streets in my city. On the other hand and on good days, I could celebrate the joy and beauty of life finding meaning and hope in spite of it all. But reading the mail on that hand-wringing day, I was stopped in my tracks.

The letter writer, Dr. Brian Blount, an African American professor and seminary president from the South, and his muse, an Old Testament prophet named Jeremiah, had collaborated: "When there is blood in the streets, when there is devastation in the land, buy property!"[1] What in this broken world were they talking about? George Floyd had just been murdered in Minneapolis; demonstrations for racial justice and police reform were happening in major cities in this country and around the world. My own city was burning, downtown windows boarded up to prevent more destruction. Buy property? Here? Now?

Both prophets, one from today and the other from ancient times, were advising their listeners to engage and invest in this mess of hopelessness. Jeremiah was a prophet in the land of Judah, a dying country with its capital, Jerusalem, under siege. The seminary president, a black man from the South who knows first-hand the ravages of racism and bigotry, is acutely aware of blood running in our own streets, of tyrants who seek to undermine democracy, of an ever-widening gap between rich and poor. Buy property? Here? Now?

This modern-day prophet and professor and his Old Testament cohort from Judah do indeed stop us in our tracks. "God has a WORD," these two holy faces say in harmony, "a word that glimmers with hope." They are not cynical; their eyes are wide open to the brokenness and still they tell of glimmering hope. "Don't sell and move away! Buy! Invest in this sorry situation." God tells Jeremiah and then reminds us that "houses and fields and vineyards shall again be bought in this land. The people who've been chased away will one day return to this land. They will reclaim it and they

1. Used with permission of Dr. Brian Blount in a letter to alumni of Union Presbyterian Seminary, Richmond, Virginia, and Charlotte, North Carolina, September 2020.

will flourish in it." The land of Judah—so decimated, its people slaughtered or running for their lives—that land, says Jeremiah, will be restored, renewed. Jeremiah and *his* modern-day muse believe that God invests in God's people, that the Holy One is a God of restoration and renewal, hope and resurrection.

And then the modern-day prophet, scholar that he is, reminds us of a well-known Bible verse many know by heart, John 3:16, words he says are often misinterpreted or co-opted to suit particular points of view or personal piety. The professor says plainly, "God invested in us by sending the man from Nazareth. Jesus' coming was God's way of buying property when there was blood running in the streets. Jesus' coming was God staking a claim, buying into the possibility that humankind could and would thrive—and that we should trust in the promise of that possibility."

The intervention of the Holy One shows *us* how to intervene. We are plagued by darkness and despair and surrounded by multiple pandemics: a culture obsessed with individualism that threatens the common good, rampant racism and classism that ensnare us all, unabashed greed for power and wealth, nationalism and political malpractice, and a massive health crisis all wreaking devastation and forcing us to live in anxiety and uncertainty. But the modern-day prophet from the South says, "Perhaps God is speaking now. Not through the pandemic but in spite of it. Not through racial injustice. But in spite of it. Because of it."

Take this to heart. Take it to mean that our words matter, that our voices need to be heard, that there are people all around with whom we can join hands to make a difference, that this God we likely understand in alternating states of shrouded mystery and concrete images is a resurrection God who is continually renewing and restoring and investing—staking claim and buying land. When there is blood in the streets and devastation in the land, when we are bowed down by anxiety and worry, buy property! Invest in hope and promise. Trust the God who comes to dwell with us in our own broken streets. Buy property! Here. Now.

REFLECTION

This modern-day prophet and his Old Testament muse stop us in our tracks. They are not cynical; their eyes are wide open and still they tell of glimmering hope.

- Name some ways you might interpret "blood in the streets and devastation in the land."
- "God has a WORD," these two holy faces say in harmony, "a word that glimmers with hope." Consider some meanings or examples of this WORD.
- What do you make of the situations Jeremiah describes and of the brokenness in our own land?
- How does God's intervention in human history show us how to intervene, engage?
- What might "buying land" look like for modern-day worriers?
- Take time to read the book of Jeremiah.

3

Breathe with me

"BREATHE WITH ME," SHE said. It was her second round of breast cancer, both times indescribable journeys testing her endurance to the limits, mentally and physically. And yet I'd rarely seen her without light in her eyes and most often, a smile. It seemed there had always been an infectious aura of peace about her, even in her dying. She loved people, exuding warmth and the joy of life, taking great pleasure in her seemingly simple life, teaching and learning, volunteering and spending as much time as she could with a wide circle of friends. She and her husband, an equally grounded and thoughtful professor in the city where we lived—she as extroverted as he was introverted, spent many days bird watching and hiking trails, tromping in the woods and tracking wildlife, keeping careful records of what they observed. Their shared passions for nature and the outdoors and especially for birds gave their life together a sense of discovery and adventure in the beautiful lake country of Minnesota—winter, spring, summer, fall—and beyond. But as the days shortened at the end of her life, after months of steady decline, we'd visit at her bedside and I'd say, "I'm here," to which she would reply, "Breathe with me," squeezing my hand in hers and absorbing the quiet peace that surrounded us.

In a grim accident in a chain of rugged mountains famous for challenging the very best mountain climbers, one of the best and most experienced fell to his death one afternoon three years ago. He was hiking across a narrow ledge on the side of a nearly vertical mountain. Whether he slipped or there was an equipment failure or a falling rock, it wasn't clear what happened. He was prepared with proper equipment, a satellite phone for communication, and he'd checked in with the rangers and his spouse prior to beginning the climb. That split moment in the mountains of western Colorado changed the entire universe for all who loved this man. He and his wife, both of them clergy, both avid outdoors people most at home in the mountains, found peace and tranquility—God's presence—in wilderness spaces.

His passion for life and the people he loved, especially people marginalized in one way or another, was not outdone by his love of nature but I suspect they competed neck in neck. As his spouse began chronicling her grief, sharing messages and posts of a loss so raw and wrenching, so shocking that only pen and paper kept her from madness, the depth of her own brokenness was haunting. "Breathe with me," she begged. "Please, breathe with me." What I remember about those raw expressions of shock and a grief I can't begin to imagine was her ability to name so graphically the depth of sorrow that became her life. He was my sister's pastor, one who exuded the joy of life, a free and passionate spirit, opinionated and fun-loving. And with so many others, my sister too was devastated by his death.

Breathe with me, I say to my own spouse when life becomes complicated. We've just experienced a spate of family health crises, diagnoses that have a way of stopping us in our tracks as we confront our own vulnerability and lack of control. When our need for predictability—for solid ground beneath our feet—is threatened, focusing on the act of breathing narrows our vision to the basics. It reminds us that breathing is all we can handle at the moment and its sufficiency has to be enough. At birth, parents wait with trepidation for newborns to inhale those first gasps of air, filling their lungs with life-giving breath so critical for life outside the womb.

Much later those same parents will say to children overcome with emotion or fear or excitement, "Take a breath." It's a way of calming ourselves.

Breathe with me, says the Holy One. Here is air, wind, spirit, life—the essence of a God who creates and sustains life. Breathing marks our dependence on the Giver of Life. It's also an invitation to mutuality asking, sometimes begging, for another's presence in stripping away the chaos to participate only in what will keep us alive, the primal act of breathing. Sometimes it's all we can do.

My family continues to mourn the death of our brother, another loss we wrestle with every day. We too are surrounded by holy faces, people who breathe with us, walk with us, remember with us. They are compassionate and empathetic, loving and supportive of a loss too deep for words. They help remind us to be careful about the ways we make sense of life, to be slow to presume we have special insights, to be less eager to make proclamations of faith and more earnest about steadfast love and grace. I see the face of God in each of them. We breathe together.

The extraordinary voice of Minnesota writer, Louise Erdrich, in her book, *The Painted Drum*, reminds us of the truth of life:

> Life will break you. Nobody can protect you from that, and living alone won't either, for solitude will also break you with its yearning. You have to love. You have to feel. It is the reason you are here on earth. You are here to risk your heart. You are here to be swallowed up. And when it happens that you are broken, or betrayed, or left, or hurt, or death brushes near, let yourself sit by an apple tree and listen to the apples falling all around you in heaps, wasting their sweetness. Tell yourself you tasted as many as you could.[1]

Louise Erdrich knows the truth of being human and vulnerable.

To love and feel and risk our hearts is the reason we are here. None of us escapes brokenness or betrayal or hurt or death. Without vulnerability, without risking one's heart, a meaningful life is not possible. When the world is falling apart before our eyes, look

1. Erdrich, *Painted Drum*, 274.

for the holy faces around you. Invite them to breathe with you. Let the spirit of the Holy One, the breath of life, fill you with wonder and peace. "If the world were going to end tomorrow, I would plant an apple tree today," declared a reflective Martin Luther. And once it has grown a bit, let yourself sit beneath that same tree listening to the apples falling all around you, wasting their sweetness as Erdrich reminds us. Then tell yourself that you tasted as many as you could. Breathe with me. The breath of life comes in all the holy faces that grace our lives, even apples in an orchard.

REFLECTION

When the world is falling apart before our eyes, look for the holy faces around you. Invite them to breathe with you. Let the spirit of the Holy One, the breath of life, fill you with wonder and peace.

- Describe a time when it felt to you as if the world were falling apart, a time of deep loss or fear.
- When have you been asked to breathe with someone? When have you needed someone to breathe with you? What was it like?
- Do you agree with Louise Erdrich that life will break us and still we have to love and feel and risk our hearts? Why or why not?
- What does it mean for you that the breath of life comes in all the holy faces that grace our lives?

4

Brutus and Friends

Among the pleasures of the summers my family and I spend in the Rocky Mountains each year are regular encounters with the animals that make their home in this stunningly beautiful part of the world. We've often felt the perceptive presence of deer who each spring seem to come closer and closer to the cabin, looking into the windows and into our eyes seeming to challenge our presence in their territory, on their turf. Often they're accompanied by newly born fawns whose protection demands unrelenting vigilance. We've been chased and challenged again and again by these beautifully delicate and sometimes aggressive creatures that clearly know this terrain to be their own and seem offended at the presence of humans.

Nature is filled with so many kinds of holy faces. When a gangly moose wanders languidly up from the river, we are mesmerized by its bulk and awkward gait, thrilled to get a close-up look at this amazing creature with its massive head and body that looks almost comical, each body part seeming to be connected with bungee cords or giant rubber bands. Foxes make their homes here too but they are more elusive. Still, we see one or two each summer coming and going from hidden dens impossible to locate. Mountain lions, or cougars as they are sometimes called, are always around but they too are stealthy and it takes skill to see them, their greenish yellow eyes glinting from trees along the river and in the forest.

But it's the bears who rule—both grizzlies and black bears—commanding a presence like no other creature. Even the deer seem to pay attention, perhaps homage, when a bear holds forth. Grizzlies generally roam higher up in the mountains but occasionally they too show up with their familiar hump and silver gray coat. Both species are given wide berth and cautious respect. A female fondly named Tillie by us humans lived for years along the river and appeared regularly in July and August to feast on huckleberries and June berries. Hungry from her long winter of hibernation, the warmth of summer and the ripening of berries was a clarion call to leave her den to forage for food. Later in August, Tillie and her family appeared more often, zealous now to replenish their reserves for the long months of winter. And each summer, bear stories make the rounds: a neighbor and his dog chased to their front door, an attack on hikers whose presence surprised a female and her cub, and occasionally a fatal attack that rocks the community and reminds everyone that this can be a wild place requiring respect and humility together with caution.

The bear story last year was our own. It was August, old Tillie seemed to be long gone, and the word along our road was that a very large male was making regular forays to the apple trees of several neighbors. We'd seen him too, often accompanied by two smaller bears. We watched with awe when he lumbered across the grassy expanse outside our windows, astonished at his size and then his speed when he became aware of our presence. But when we woke one night to hear the crack of breaking branches and deep, rumbling breathing coming from a mountain ash tree at the edge of our property, we were wide awake. Over the course of the next two or three weeks, we watched warily as Brutus built a massive nest in the center of that large mountain ash, making his claim just beyond "our" property line. We could see his enormous head and face clearly as he pawed one berry-laden branch after another, quickly stripping the berries, breaking huge branches to add to the ever-growing heft of his nest—while watching us as attentively as we watched him. Finally, when it became clear that Brutus was not a temporary visitor come to sample apples or berries, authorities had to be called for help. The mountain ash tree was being destroyed by a ravenous bear whose daily chorus of breaking branches and heavy breathing no longer seemed entertaining. And it wasn't safe to be outside.

Two "bear and lion specialists" from the Department for Fish and Wildlife first made a foray around the road and along the river trying to spot their prey. But Brutus seemed to know instinctively when they were coming and before their arrival, he would suddenly disappear. Then the two men brought a long, tube-shaped metal trap on a flatbed trailer complete with a trap door made to fall when curious wildlife could not resist the odorous lure of deer hindquarters and opened cans of tuna placed inside. Perhaps they should have used berries. They parked the trap among the broken branches below the mountain ash, right where Brutus took his daily and nightly leaps into the arms of the tree. They'd spotted the two smaller bears nearby and stunned them so they could be transported safely to more remote quarters in the surrounding mountains. They hoped to do the same with this three- or four-hundred-pound specimen.

But Brutus was no specimen and he was not about to be captured. We watched and waited for days for his return. Two plus weeks of gazing at us from his tree perch as he feasted on berries and branches had begun to feel almost neighborly. I'd grown strangely fond of him and silently cheered his shrewd ability to avoid capture. We'd watched him for hours to keep track of his whereabouts and to make sure he was "staying put." His constant gaze was mesmerizing and though it didn't diminish our caution, it felt as if he thought he'd come home. That face and those eyes communicated something primal: "I belong here."

But the canny Brutus seemed to be long gone, not tempted in the least by the reeking morsels left to lure him into the bear trap below his nest. I imagined him alerting all the other wild creatures, a confab in the woods along the river, the earnest faces of bears, deer, and fox, and those elusive mountain lions discussing their dominion and protecting one another. Soon we too would leave, making our own nest for winter-hibernating in warmer climes. Perhaps Brutus the wise was showing us the truth of the wild places, sending us on our way after looking us in the eye to remind us that the wild ones too are holy creatures, that this too is *their* home.

Be aware when the deer come close protecting their young or a fox runs silently beneath the trees. Listen if you are able to the birds when they call at daybreak. Enjoy their uncommon beauty. And if you are privileged to look into the face of a beautiful black bear as it builds its own winter nest, watch in wonder and awe and respect. Nature is filled with many kinds of holy faces.

REFLECTION

Nature is filled with many kinds of holy faces.

- How might nature be a place of wonder or awe for you?
- Think of a time when you've looked into the face of an animal and felt some connection. Describe what it was like.
- Is it too much a stretch to regard the presence, the faces of animals or birds or insects or mountains or deserts or islands, as holy? Why or why not?
- Read *Martin Marten* by Brian Doyle.

5

Chestnuts from Childhood

"Do you see what I see?" It's a question meant to elicit curiosity and from my earliest days of childhood, I made friends easily with anyone whose love of surprise or beauty or imagination equaled my own. "Look, look! Out there beyond the kelp patch, do you see what I see?" and swiveling from our ever-present search for seashells and agates and beach glass, I'd squint against the light reflecting off the bay to discover fins, their sleek black knife-edge slipping through the saltwater like miniature submarines. On occasion, we'd see the faces of the porpoise and whales that ply the waters of the inland sound where I grew up. Sometimes they'd come near enough so that we'd hear the blow of rushing breath as they surfaced, forcefully exhaling before taking in oxygen. Sometimes we'd see the spraying spout of seawater and orca breath. But often their faces were elusive as they played gracefully, rolling out along the kelp line just beyond the beach. The mysteries of their existence, their enormous size, their very being sparked wonder and awe. We saw them often.

In a similar way, I suppose, is another of my childhood discoveries, this one on land on a nearby island where in the summer and fall we'd take walks. Whether the trees were the nearly extinct American chestnut or some other variety of chestnut tree, their canopies seemed to shade entire blocks of the neighborhood. Perhaps because they were so large and their fruit so beautiful, they took on a mythical quality. After the flowering and growth of a hard, green, prickly shell—the better to protect its lovely treasure inside, the heavy orbs bigger than a walnut would fall to the ground below the massive trees. I don't know if the discovery of that beautiful chestnut inside the ugly, spiky shell was my own or something shown to me by playmates. But either way, it was a magnificent discovery. For every round, hard ball that fell from the glorious chestnut tree contained a shiny, mahogany-like slightly irregular ball. It looked like a well-polished piece of fine wood, something precious and unique, hardly what one would expect looking at the ugly shell that had protected it.

We knew not to eat them, which may suggest that they were horse chestnuts rather than the sweet chestnut grown for consumption. But it wasn't about eating them. We collected them in bags and small boxes. We polished their already sleek surfaces and placed them in bowls. The chestnuts from my childhood were treasures after all, mahogany gems fit for the finest table, not to be consumed or tasted but to be noticed. Those chestnuts from my childhood were among the first treasures I found in nature, among the first possessions I collected. That they fell from trees and were free was miracle enough. But their rich hues of darkest brown and deep wine-red and their lovely gloss satisfied my eyes, my spirit. I think of them still, their luster and sheen a holy face so pleasing to look at and to hold. They've become a metaphor for lifelong appreciation of the riches of nature and miracle of trees, the beauty of wood and color. They are another of the "chestnuts from my childhood" that strike me as holy.

Nature by its very ubiquity is the palette against which all of creation is on exhibition. We humans often understand ourselves to be the "crown" of creation or some other lofty notion of exalted status or inherent superiority. When I read a book by Brian Doyle or a poem by Mary Oliver or an essay by Parker J. Palmer, I find in all of them a reverence for creation, often focused on inanimate beings, though "beings" seems to be a word we claim primarily for the human family, even calling this personification. From my Oregon home, I look to the mountain Brian Doyle describes as a creature, a body that connects with other creatures, animate and inanimate, that communicates and holds forth, showing all of creation to be holy, sacred. When Doyle writes about a bird, a raven named Moses who talks and tells jokes and is a companion to a seaside village of animals and people and places all of whom communicate with one another, he captures the wonder of holy faces in all their animate and inanimate creaturely-ness.

Mary Oliver welcomes the sun each morning, writing "Hello, sun in my face, Hello, you who make the morning and spread it over the fields and into the faces of the tulips . . . and into the windows of, even, the miserable and the crotchety—best preacher that ever was, dear star . . . that just happens to hold us in the great hands of light."[1] In response to Mary Oliver, Parker J. Palmer reminds us to live life fiercely, all of life, all of creation.[2] And when we watch the news, whether it's another story of war and the destruction of a beautiful country like Ukraine or heart-wrenching reports from Turkey about a massive earthquake's ability to annihilate whole swaths of people and property, go beyond your own broken heart to act and support every effort to affirm life and the beauty of all creation.

From my childhood, I've watched another holy mountain, another volcano whose power to erupt could be life-threatening and destructive. It too is a holy face, an anchor connecting me to my people and my place. It too is part of a chain of mountains teeming with abundant life and energy, a home for all creatures. There it sits, its familiar shape altered only by the amount of snowfall that covers it in winter or the way it reflects the sun on a summer evening, another "chestnut from childhood." It supplies much-needed water and recreation, nourishes creatures great and small, and is a feast of beauty and a sign of home. On the beach beneath my feet there are seashells of many shapes and shades,

1. Oliver, "Why I Wake Early," 171.
2. Palmer, "My Heart Is Broken."

some broken, some whole, their iridescent surfaces shiny from a tide just going out. Walking along the shoreline in the places where agates are most visible, my eyes catch a glimmer of refracted light leading me to a tiny nugget of agate, a "tear drop" and the choicest find for agate lovers. I add it to the collection in my pocket. It will end up in a large glass jar, joining so many others found along that curving shoreline. Up above the driftwood-strewn beach are moss-covered logs, thick and lacy green blankets that thrive in the shade and moist surroundings of a Pacific Northwest island.

Hello, chestnut tree and chestnuts from childhood. Hello, moss and moss-covered log. Hello, Mount Hood and Mount Baker. Hello, golden agate, massive whale, and playful porpoise. "Do you see what I see?" You are part of the wonder of this beautiful planet, this ever-expanding universe we share. From childhood onward, you have shaped my world and shown me the many faces of God. So many holy faces.

REFLECTION

The natural world and its very ubiquity is a palette where all of creation is on exhibition.

- Do you resonate to the sun as "the best preacher that ever was" or a raven named Moses? Why or why not do you appreciate the personification of inanimate things?
- What patterns in nature help illumine God/Allah/Yahweh/ the Holy One for you?
- Describe some of the "chestnuts from childhood" that have marked your life or expanded your understanding of holy faces.

6

Desmond Tutu

> We are made for goodness. We are made for love. We are made for friendliness. We are made for togetherness. We are made for all of the beautiful things that you and I know. We are made to tell the world that there are no outsiders. All are welcome: black, white, yellow, rich, poor, educated, not educated, male, female, gay, straight, all, all, all. We all belong to this family, this human family, God's family. —Desmond Tutu

How does one begin to honor so holy a face as that of Desmond Tutu? Where even to begin? I shall go back to the beginning, to a story told by this extraordinary human being known around the world about an incident from his childhood. He was being interviewed by the BBC, and the interviewer asked Tutu to identify the defining moment in his life. He paused only a second or two and then began: he was nine years old, walking with his mother along a dusty road in Klerksdorp, a town in the Transvaal region of South Africa. It was one of the first Dutch settlements in the Transvaal and Tutu's family knew the daily humiliations of being poor and black. As he and his mother walked, a tall white man dressed in a black suit came towards them. Before nine-year-old Desmond or his mother could step from the footpath to the gutter—a sign of submission—the white man stepped down into the gutter and tipped his hat to them in a gesture of respect.

Tutu told the BBC that the white man was an Anglican priest, Trevor Huddleston, someone known for his opposition to the evils of apartheid. When nine-year-old Tutu stood on that footpath that day looking up at his mother in disbelief, she told him the white man was a man of God. I picture Tutu's cherubic nine-year-old face as he absorbed this act, later claiming his own calling: "I want to be a man of God and an Anglican priest." And indeed, Huddleston became for him a mentor and model in Tutu's own opposition to apartheid and to the unequivocal equality of all human beings. To identify *the* defining moment in one's life with such clarity and conviction underscores extraordinary prescience. That singular act of respect on the part of a white man would provide the backdrop for Desmond Tutu's entire life. For him, the power of that act shaped a lifelong premise that influenced everything he did and everything he accomplished: every human being is made in the image of God.[1]

The endearing face of nine-year old Desmond seemed to follow him—even into old age. His eyes were riveting, brilliant; he was quick, mentally and physically, always exhibiting a hint of playfulness that belied his deadly serious commitments and mission in life. And his diminutive physical size contradicted a towering and powerful presence both in South Africa and around the world. In spite of, and perhaps because of the suffering of his people (and all people living under subjugation), he exuded light and love and joy that no doubt contributed to the archbishop's unforgettable countenance. His was a holy face revealing unconditional love and steely single-mindedness. That single-mindedness called to account both the state and the church and he quickly became an exemplary icon for the anti-apartheid movement, a voice in South Africa and far beyond. For his prophetic, erudite, and unrelenting voice for justice and equality, he was awarded the Nobel Peace Prize in 1984.

1. This story is taken from The Grouped Churches, "Asked by the BBC . . ."

One of my favorite images is a well-known photo I've saved—taken on stage after a speaking event sometime before he retired. An ever-present smile on his face, the archbishop's arms are flung high in the air, his bishop's cross askew as he dances—one foot in the air, bouncing on the other, his red alb flying around him as floodlights light up the faces of a large audience watching in delight. The words of Sufi poet Hafiz accompany the picture. I doubt there is a more apt description of Desmond Tutu:

Created for Joy

I sometimes forget
that I was created for Joy.
My mind is too busy.
My Heart is too heavy
for me to remember
that I have been
called to dance
the Sacred dance of life.

I was created to smile
to Love
To be lifted up
And to lift others up.

O, Sacred One
Untangle my feet
from all that ensnares.
Free my soul
that we might
Dance
and that our dancing
might be contagious.[2]

Desmond Tutu's passion for justice and equality was contagious indeed. He seemed to absorb and somehow magnify the energy of others who shared his longing for freedom and his irrepressible spirit. His capacity for unconditional love was voracious

2. Weinmann, "I Sometimes Forget."

and exuberant, fueling and empowering others to join him in defying the subjugation of his people. In 1995 when the Truth and Reconciliation Commission was established in South Africa to help bring about reconciliation and forgiveness, witnesses identified as perpetrators and as victims of torture and other forms of suppression described the abuse in public hearings. Archbishop Tutu chaired those hearings and I remember his powerful words about the healing power of forgiveness as one atrocity after another was shared. "In forgiving, people are not being asked to forget. On the contrary, it is important to remember, so that we should not let such atrocities happen again. Forgiveness does not mean condoning what has been done. It means taking what happened seriously and not minimizing it; drawing out the sting in the memory that threatens to poison our entire existence."[3] For Desmond Tutu, forgiveness was the way we heal the world.

Archbishop Tutu died in 2021 but his exuberant spirit and capacity for love and forgiveness are gifts that will not be forgotten. He truly embodied the love of the God he proclaimed.

> *The man who contained it all may rest, but the love of God that danced this earth, the justice of God that rang round this earth, the joy of God that laughed on this earth: these are attributes of God that do not die. We choose only whether they will live on in us or die in us. Thank you, Archbishop Desmond Tutu, for teaching us the meaning of God's love.*[4]

REFLECTION

Desmond Tutu's life exuded unconditional love and steely single-mindedness. His presence as an erudite prophet and voice for justice and equality is exemplary.

- Describe your own memories of Desmond Tutu. What images come to mind?

3. Tutu, *No Future without Forgiveness*, 271.
4. Hoster, "Man Who Contained . . ." Used with permission.

- Which attributes named by Sufi poet, Hafiz, most capture the spirit of this man?
- Desmond Tutu truly embodied the love of the God he proclaimed. In what ways did he hold accountable both the church and the state?
- The injustices of our world cry out for leaders like Desmond Tutu. Are there others whose prophetic and courageous voices have marked your life and/or the lives of their communities? Name them. Give thanks for them. Be inspired by them.

7

Helen Jane

PERHAPS HELEN JANE, AS she refers to herself, would not approve of being included in a book called *Holy Faces*. And I shall surely ask her permission before presuming to describe and hopefully honor this remarkable human being, my dear friend Helen (as I call her). It isn't that she shirks from praise or respect and appreciation; she simply is herself, matter-of-fact, gracious, and practical. And it is not her bent to consider herself in any way unusual or particularly set apart. But for most who know her including her own large family, Helen Jane is a presence whose spirit brings light and life to whatever situation she encounters, to whomever she is with, and wherever she is. Helen, now ninety-eight years old, is extraordinary and truly a holy face.

Growing up in the Midwest, she knew the grounded ethos of her Scandinavian roots. With her brother and sisters, all of them long-lived, she attended St. Olaf College in Minnesota earning a degree in music. Music at St. Olaf, including singing in their renowned choir, was life-changing for Helen. After marrying and following her spouse into the public life of a pastoral calling, she and her beloved Al began their own large family. Over the course of a dozen years or more, three daughters and three sons were born to them, all of them growing up in southern California. An accomplished pianist and organist, Helen taught music and served as organist and musician for many churches and organizations—decades-long stints that continued into her nineties when she felt the time had come to play only for herself. But music is only one of her passions.

Helen's devotion to her large and scattered family includes spouses, past and present, talented grandchildren, and like every family, differing lifestyles and ways of doing things. She helped rear independent and accomplished children, none of whom were perfect or without the usual baggage that makes parents both crazy or terrified and happy and proud. Along the way, she and Al found an idyllic lakeside cabin in the mountains of western Montana where they and their lively tribe spent summer vacations. This Montana foray left indelible marks on all six children and together with Helen and Al (who died several years ago), four of them have come "home" with their own families, retiring as their parents did among the stunningly beautiful mountains and lakes of northwestern Montana.

Three years ago, Helen Jane's children were concerned about her living alone in the home she'd enjoyed for many years. It was pandemic time and the isolation worried them. Helen wasn't chafing about isolation; she simply made the best of it even though it was challenging. Together with her children, neighbors and her church community watched out for her just as she watched out for them. But she was now nearly ninety-six and so with one of her daughters who'd recently moved from California to her own Montana patch of paradise, Helen and Mary began to investigate tiny houses. Mary's small farm in the country seemed a good location for Helen's need for independence, for Mary's watchful eye, and for the pleasure of both mother and daughter. With help from the whole family, Helen moved into her tiny house on Mary's property midsummer. It was a big transition, not without losses and not without much planning and ongoing adjustments. Many friends worried, wondering if this would be a wise move. Helen Jane likely did too but once she had decided this made sense, she plowed ahead and with family help settled into her new retreat just across the yard from Mary's house.

There among the gardens and studio, the alpacas and chickens and pets and bed and breakfast digs, Helen—helped by Mary and her other children—has made her tiny house into a home. She and Mary found furnishings and turned a small upstairs loft into a mini-library and space for a guest. One son-in-law built an attached covered deck where Helen and her little dog entertain visitors outside on sunny days. Helen's friends come to visit, making sure that her upbeat reports are indeed accurate, missing her while finding her spunk and spirit exemplary. Once the isolation of the pandemic began to lift, she invited her spiritual formation group to gather with her at 6:30 a.m., a years-long morning habit at Helen's former home. Grandchildren and nieces and nephews, adults themselves now, come from around the country to see her.

Out in the countryside now, many miles from her former home and much-loved church family, Helen Jane made the decision not to drive any longer, another loss she accepted with grace. Now without her spacious old home and ability to be mobile and independent, Helen shows no sign of regret nor does she lament what is lost or her old age. She continues to find joy in all the activity at Mary's farm—the visits from friends and relatives, pleasure at participating in weddings and birthdays and parties hosted by Mary, family gatherings and daily life with animals all around. She relished the first snowfall, even receiving the gift of new snowshoes from her daughters at Christmastime, then snowshoeing together later in the winter.

From her bedroom windows, she watches the vast night sky and its canopy of stars during long winter nights, noting the changes as the earth rotates around the sun and describing with wonder the beauty of each season. Helen's appreciation for nature and her gifts of hospitality continue to find new outlets at Mary's farm, helping with gardening and cooking and hosting parties and welcoming a steady flow of visitors winter and summer. Her curiosity and spirit of openhearted warmth create strong relationships with nearly everyone she meets. Helen Jane loves people.

An inveterate reader and astute observer, she converses readily about politics and global events. Always at home in the church, she's had to accept not being able to travel the distance to her much-loved parish of the last years. She does this with typical pragmatism and grace even as she continues to be invited and transported to special events and to local symphony concerts and plays. Helen has been an avid sports fan since her days as a young mother in California—she knows the players and statistics and rarely misses watching her favorite teams. Always the learner and willing to tackle technology, she uses her computer, iPhone, radio, and television every day.

Helen Jane reflects the goodness of life and the grace of a good God. She is ageless. But she's also a realist, clear-eyed about loss and grief and suffering, clear-eyed and outspoken about things political and religious. She is not a Pollyanna or one who reflects all sweetness and positivity. She is compassionate to a fault. Helen's holy face and holy life inspire and enrich all who know her and her long life continues to be a gift of immeasurable worth and inestimable joy.

REFLECTION

Helen Jane is a presence whose spirit brings light and life to whatever situation she encounters, to whomever she is with, wherever she is. She is an extraordinary human being.

- Do you know someone like Helen? Describe this person and their impact on you.
- What are some of the characteristics you most admire about a person like Helen?
- Are there aspects of this kind of person you find confusing or challenging?
- What does it mean to you that Helen Jane reflects the goodness of life and the grace of a good God?

8

Holy Mother

THE FIRST TIME I heard English rock and blues guitarist Eric Clapton sing "Holy Mother" with Luciano Pavarotti, I knew I was listening to more than two extraordinary artists perform a beautiful song.[1] Clapton, regarded as one of the most gifted and influential guitarists of all time, begins his soulful plea with a riveting beat of chords and the pathos of his own voice. When world-renowned Italian tenor, Luciano Pavarotti, begins to sing, the urgency and depth of their mournful cry becomes a universal prayer to Mary, mother of Jesus, the holy mother. In the song's opening chords and lyrics, one hears more than haunting music and evocative words. The syncopated rhythm, passion, and aching honesty resonate at the deepest level. A rather incongruous pair of artists so different from one another raise their voices in heartfelt longing, begging the Holy Mother to show up while describing their own brokenness, their own unbearable despair. Clapton is grieving the death of a beloved band member and his own precipitous descent into alcohol and drugs. His pain is palpable and the music is powerful, especially as Pavarotti riffs into the sorrow, his magnificent voice making rapt listeners erupt with unabashed emotion.

1. See https://www.youtube.com/watch?v=x9uYu4R2nk8.

Their pleas reverberate with a longing for peace of mind and release from pain. I've listened to the song dozens of times and it never gets old. Yes, the artists are brilliant and the music dazzling. Their faces, their body language, their presence all are spellbinding. But my enchantment goes deeper . . . there is familiarity with this holy mother, maternal accessibility, perhaps even personal acquaintance felt by both Clapton and Pavarotti. The power of their song is a tribute, a testament to the holy mother. And for me, it taps into a long-held yearning for more meaningful exegesis—interpretation and symbolism—of the person of Mary, the mother of Jesus, another holy one.

My longing has to do with the centrality of women, our significance and uniqueness, the power and potency of femaleness, and our generative role as birth-makers and life-givers. Praying to Mary has not been part of my faith formation. Not wanting to elevate Mary or grant her sacred, God-like status, my tradition tends to make the mother of Jesus a secondary character in the biblical story—an ordinary girl from Nazareth, chosen, obedient, faithful. But female. And so to hear this holy mother venerated and sought out in the plaintive prayer of a rock singer and his famous Italian friend is both jarring and life-giving. The song they sing is a declaration, a pronouncement: this woman is the holy mother! God has chosen a peasant woman, still a teenager, to bear a child. And not just any child but another holy one, Jesus the Christ, called by Christians the son of God. Suddenly Mary's role as a birth-giver, a mother, a female is no longer understated or subordinate. Created herself in the image of God, she becomes the vehicle for bearing God to the world. Holy mother indeed!

Of course Mary of Nazareth has been celebrated over the centuries by so many writers and poets and musicians who have written and sung their Ave Marias and Magnificats. But our patriarchal culture has continued to affirm male dominance, male control, male authority. This maleness includes mostly male references for God and hierarchical images of the universe. Roman Catholics have elevated Mary in their tradition but still refuse to ordain women as priests. The halls of Congress, businesses and board rooms are slowly integrating. Still we wait for a first female head of state in our country. In my denomination and others, women finally are sought-after pastors and bishops, authoritative voices across the church. But it's taken a very long time.

Eric Clapton's lyrics describe the holy mother as one who waits to embrace his troubled soul, to hold and comfort him in his unbearable grief. She is accessible, a steady presence who knows herself to be an earth-maker, a pain-bearer, a life-giver. And yet this holy mother is earthy and ordinary. She tends the animals and her garden and vineyards feed her family. With compassion and worry, she watches her son grow into manhood. Heartache and sorrow will come soon enough. Perhaps it is her humanness and her strength that draw us.

Luciano Pavarotti's booming proclamation of this holy mother resonates with power and his own largess. We are left with no doubt about her ability to embrace the brokenhearted, lift up the voiceless, and break the bonds of injustice. I imagine my daughters and theirs stomping their feet and shouting, "I am woman. Hear me roar!" I look at a photo of newly-elected women bishops finding many familiar faces whose lineage is my own. I am inspired by their perseverance and honored by their determination.

With Clapton and Pavarotti, it's impossible not to feel the agony in their words and the resonance of their voices together with their iron-clad trust in the holy mother. Holy Mother, wrap us all in your loving arms. Empower and stir us up to care for one another; to care for our mother the earth, so in need of restoration. Holy mother, inspire and give us courage to work for justice and peace, acting on behalf of the voiceless poor and all who struggle with losses too deep for words. Holy mother, make us in your image and hear our prayer!

REFLECTION

Clapton and Pavarotti share an ability to name unbearable grief and unrelenting suffering while venerating the holy mother and her power to heal. Yes, the artists are brilliant and the music dazzling. But my enchantment goes deeper . . . there is familiarity with this holy mother, maternal accessibility, perhaps even personal acquaintance . . . The power of their song is a tribute, a testament to the holy mother.

- Take time to listen to this rendition of "Holy Mother." It can be found at https://www.youtube.com/watch?v=x9uYu4R2nk8.
- Which words in the song do you find most meaningful?
- Describe your experience or understanding of Mary, the mother of Jesus.
- Do you resonate to the power of this song? Why or why not?
- How might you pay tribute to the holy mother, honoring her role as the mother of Jesus?

9

Hummingbirds

"They're baaack!" I shout one afternoon in late spring. I've just heard the unmistakable whirring sound and sensed the erratic flutter of a tiny hummingbird darting among the branches of a nearby tree. The sound and motion of its wings beating up to an astonishing eighty times per second has once again caught my attention as this uniquely amazing little bird makes its first appearance after a long winter. Darting from branch to branch in an old pine tree, it is hard to follow as it seeks out much-needed nourishment. Soon it flits around the house to the other side of the yard where flowering annuals, newly planted in colorful pots, offer sweet nectar and life-giving sustenance. The amazing thing is that we know these captivating creatures return year after year, remembering the very places where they spend summers, remembering the flowers and blossoming trees and how long it takes for each blossom to refill, perhaps remembering even the humans who delight in their presence as they "come home" yet again.

That coming "home" or migration is as mind-boggling as the birds themselves. They seem to be able to fly thousands of miles without food or rest and they are the smallest long-distance migrants in the world. Making their summer residence as far north as southern Alaska and wintering in warmer climates nearer the equator, they instinctively know home only in the western hemisphere, from southern Chile to Alaska. These minute birds, measuring from two to six inches depending on the species,[1] are yet another of God's extraordinary creatures that inspire awe and wonder, another of creation's holy faces.

The presence of hummingbirds in spring is always a portent of summer. Its miniature body including its beautifully colored head and throat shimmers with life as it ushers in a new season each year. Where I live, I've learned to recognize the red-headed Anna's, the Calliope, and the Rufous. But the hummingbird family is large, around 350 species (and counting),[2] giving us ample opportunity to learn more about them, how to enjoy them, and—most important—how to protect and care for them as global warming threatens their existence. They're the only bird species that can fly backwards.[3] They can twist their wings approximately 200 degrees, creating lift in both the upstroke and the downstroke.[4] They can see ultraviolet light[5] and their metabolism is "nearly 100 times faster than that of an elephant."[6] Researchers describe torpor in hummingbirds as their ability to lower their body heat, allowing them to conserve energy while sleeping.[7] A hummingbird's flight muscles make up 25–30 percent of their total body weight.[8] They can fly thirty miles per hour and they dive up to sixty miles per hour.[9] And perhaps a little known fact: hummingbirds have weak feet and cannot walk very well.[10]

I wait each year for the appearance of these tiniest of creatures, for the whirring of their wings and the flitting of their small,

1. Vanover, "Hummingbird Size," para. 4.
2. Bergeson, "How Much Do Hummingbirds Weigh," para. 1.
3. "12 Most Interesting Facts," para. 6.
4. "12 Most Interesting Facts," para. 8.
5. "12 Most Interesting Facts," para. 35.
6. "12 Most Interesting Facts," para. 9.
7. See Pinkstone, "Hummingbirds Can Drop."
8. Mayntz, "35 Fun Facts about Hummingbirds," para. 8.
9. Mayntz, "35 Fun Facts about Hummingbirds," paras. 27–28.
10. See Wilde, "Do Hummingbirds Have Feet."

dynamic bodies. I feel as if I know them. And yet they are elusive, hiding their nests and themselves even as they entertain and perform. I am more than curious about their ability to survive and migrate, to remember and communicate with one another and with the humans with whom they grace their presence. They are known for flying around people's heads when feeders are empty or diving precipitously if a group of people threatens their space. Flying backward, forward, and upside down, they seem to know instinctively what we humans sometimes forget: we are all dependent on one another, connected and interconnected in ways that baffle the imagination, ways too easily forgotten or ignored by human arrogance, human preoccupation.

Many species are threatened by the changes in climate and organizations like the Audubon Society encourage us to pay attention not only to climatic change but to pesticides that kill, to urbanization, logging practices, and agricultural threats. These major dangers pose serious survival challenges for the whip-smart hummingbird. Their breeding and nesting grounds need to be protected and as with so many other creatures, hummingbird survival depends on careful attention and human action including support for natural habitats.

I keep three photographs of newly hatched hummingbird babies in my collection of pictures; their parents seem to have made themselves scarce and are nowhere to be seen. The first photo, taken by a discreet park ranger, shows a tiny nest the size of a quarter made of lacy, multicolored lichen where three indistinguishable hatchlings nestle together. In the next picture, they are distinct and recognizable and in the third, their lovely iridescent faces and brilliant throats graze the edge of the nest as they prepare to fly. Posing there as if waiting to be noticed or perhaps gathering up courage to leave their familiar nest, the beauty of these awe-inspiring creatures takes my breath away. Their lives will be marked by a constant search for food, by journeys unimaginable, and perhaps by wonder and joy as well. How privileged we are to enjoy their holy faces!

REFLECTION

I wait each year for the appearance of these tiniest of creatures. I feel as if I know them and yet they are elusive, mysterious.

- Describe your own familiarity with hummingbirds.
- What about hummingbirds do you find most captivating?
- Consider this: "Flying backward, forward, and upside down, they seem to know instinctively what we humans sometimes forget: we are all dependent on one another, connected and interconnected in ways that baffle the imagination, ways too easily forgotten or ignored by human arrogance."
- What does it mean to be dependent on one another, connected and interconnected? Do you resonate to this idea of interdependence with creatures like birds, animals, insects? Why or why not?

10

Julian, O Julian!

I PICTURE YOU, SAINTED sister, peering out from your tiny one-room cell attached to a church in Norwich, England. Perhaps it is the only image we have of you (and of course it's not a picture so much as an imagined image). But to visualize you living in that cramped and isolating anchorage is hauntingly disturbing. That you are there because you have found safe space during a lifetime of war and a plague that wreaked incalculable suffering and death across Eurasia and North Africa might be one interpretation. But we know from the riches of your writings and the power of your "showings" (visions) that you endured and flourished in that incommodious space during one of the most difficult times in human history. Some even say of you that your wisdom and keen observations about the mystical presence of God, both within and without in your fraught world, were prescient and beyond our wildest imaginings.

This is what prompts me to consider your holy face, your voice that speaks with such authority and riveting insight from your perch in the darkest days of fourteenth-century England all the way to our own time in the twenty-first century. How can that be? Surrounded by ravaging war that lasted longer than your entire life and in the chaos of the Black Plague that killed millions upon millions of people on three continents, you wrote and ministered from your pulpit/home with words and actions that continue to empower and inform our lives today. From your life in medieval times you somehow found a loving God, a God who sacrifices and suffers, a gracious and transcendent presence that cannot be reduced to our often stunted attempts to define the holy presence. In your communing with this Holy One, you have given us profound images, numinous interpretations, and life-changing understandings of the Creator and the meanings of creation. You have shown us a God of oneness who is both mother and father, a God embodied in nature, a holy presence within each of us, a God that permeates all that is.

And yet to us moderns so smitten with our own wisdom and arrogant to a fault, your world seems primitive, a world without the benefits of education or the knowledge of a limitless universe, or the power of the atom or the microchip. Your world was under siege just as ours is and yet you in your extraordinary circumstances found God within and without. You lived a life steeped in sacrificial love and grace informed by experiences, visions, and prophetic revelations. And you wrote it all down so that we might find transformation and resurrection and abundant life in our own time.

Julian, O Julian, I feel your presence as I write all these centuries later. The world I know is entrenched in one war after another. Death seems to lurk here even as it did in the Middle Ages. Injustice, fear and discrimination, and the stranglehold of power and violence continue to divide and impose their tenacious grip on so much of the world. We moderns sometimes feel as if we too live isolated in our own tiny anchorages, our own safe ports where we hope for visions and assurances of a holy presence—the spirit of a loving God—but are too blind to see. We too want to be safe and engaged in the world even as we shelter in isolation. We too know the power of love, the challenges of sacrifice, connectedness to others and to all of creation. We long for peace in the world and for the palpable presence of the spirit we understand God to be. We know our lives are connected to yours and to every other bit of life, animate and inanimate, beyond time and history.

Deep in our psyches, we sense these things you showed us from your visions and experiences of life to be true. We want to understand the meanings of creation, incarnation and resurrection, of life and death, of God. We want to experience your wisdom about the interrelatedness of all things, the oneness of life, the immeasurable power of love and sacrifice, the intertwining of every created thing. We too want to know God. You were surrounded by death in your life and yet you were also surrounded by life, embodying the very love and sacrifice you understood God to be. You are with us today and perhaps we were with you all those centuries ago as well. You were and are a source of comfort and peace, of wisdom and grace and insight.

On a shelf above my desk is a small collection of acorns—some old, some broken, always a couple of new ones from the most recent season of "acorn-making," and a large, beautifully carved wooden specimen, a gift from a woman who found Julian of Norwich as captivating as I do. They remind me of the lesson Julian taught as she considered a hazelnut, "God made it, God loves it, God keeps it." She also continues to teach us the vastness of God's mysterious and sometimes mystical identity and presence together with the intimacy of God in our own waking and sleeping, in our breathing and eating and living of life. Perhaps you, like me, sometimes are overwhelmed by the chaos and trouble that seem to characterize so much of life. It's easy for us to lament the times in which we live. But life during the Middle Ages was nothing short of catastrophic. Death was rampant and the ravages of the Hundred Years' War were unspeakable. Out of that darkness, this visionary woman invites us to new understandings of who we are, who and what God is, and what the world is like. She turns our narrow and dangerously limited views of God, ourselves, and the universe we inhabit, upside down.

Julian's discerning writings astound and astonish, her words and her imagery astute testimony to mindfulness we may envy. That she could write and contemplate as she did in her medieval world and speak to us in our time and place is nothing short of amazing.

In Julian's words, "we are God's dream, [his] homiest home."[1] Julian, O Julian, may we moderns catch a glimpse of your profoundly life-changing revelations. May we experience the clarity of your words and the power of your visions to embody a loving God in our own time. May we truly become God's dream and God's homiest home!

REFLECTION

Julian's discerning writings and visions astound and astonish. That she could write and contemplate as she did in her medieval world and speak to us in our time and place is nothing short of amazing.

- Julian's life in a tiny anchorage in Norwich, England seems to have given her extraordinary insights that resonate for us so many centuries later. What most captivates you about her wisdom?
- In what ways do Julian's visions give you hope?
- Julian believes that God is all love and then speaks of our drawing back from this notion of the unrelenting love of God. What do you make of this? Do you agree or disagree?
- What does it mean to you that we are God's dream, God's homiest home?

1. Julian of Norwich, quoted in Pennington, *Listening*, 20.

11

Loved into Being

Take one moment each day to be totally silent and consider all those people who have loved you into being. This invitation was given by Fred Rogers in his acceptance speech for a Lifetime Achievement Award at the 24th Annual Daytime Emmys for his work in a well-known children's television program, *Mister Roger's Neighborhood.*[1] In his profoundly wise way, Fred Rogers became an iconic American role model for showing us the necessity of love and the lifelong challenge it is. Without a lot of words or maxims for living a meaningful life, without being trite or naive, Mr. Rogers was exhibit one for showing viewers, both children and adults, the necessity of learning to love. He exuded kindness, respect, and authentic interest and curiosity in others and in life generally. What does it mean to be *loved into being*?

It's a rocky road, this business of being loved, of learning to love. For all the ways we dilute the many meanings of love, sometimes rendering it banal and even meaningless, it truly is the primal and primary function of the Creator, our very lifeblood, and the center of religious life as well. For Jews and Christians, the love of God is a narrative between God and God's beloved. It is central in Islam and core to practicing Buddhism which believes love to

1. See Emmy Awards, "Fred Rogers Acceptance Speech," 1:44–2:11.

be the path to freedom. In Jainism, the highest forms of love are nonviolence, sociability, compassion, and peaceful coexistence. For Baha'i, there is the love that flows from God to humans, the love humans have for God, for themselves, and for others. And yet love often seems elusive and often is among the most worn of words. How many movies have been made of love stories? How many poems written, songs composed, books published? And still we are hard at it, trying to decipher the power and emotion of love, its complexities, and the conundrum of its many meanings.

Before we bleed dry such a word and all it means, let us begin with a basic premise: love and the emotions that go with it are among the most fundamental of life's gifts. There are a million reasons why love is a spiritual principle and perhaps it isn't banal at all to take to heart what *loved into being* means in the journey of our lives. As newborns, we are desperately in need of human touch, our five senses casting about in mutual competition for signs of love. Studies by the thousands confirm the importance of swaddling a newborn child with tender care, holding and feeding, protecting and speaking words of affection, acting literally to sustain a child's very life. Fred Rogers knew this. For some, he may have seemed a simple soul; in reality he was a brilliant pastoral presence helping all of us see the foundational underpinnings of healthy life, our need to love and to be loved. His quiet ability to create and maintain authentic relationships was the love he proclaimed. Love was a constant theme in *Mister Roger's Neighborhood*, the spiritual principle that helps us discover a sense of our shared humanity.

Good parents and grandparents, good teachers and caregivers work hard to make sure every child in their care knows and feels love. They understand our need for acceptance and compassion, our human longing to be recognized. They know that affection and belonging are central to our well-being and without this affirmation, we wither and then shrivel into broken and sometimes destructive human beings. *Loved into being* means learning to love ourselves so that we are secure within ourselves, freely loving and forgiving and embracing ourselves in order to love and embrace others. Love is putting the best light on the other, knowing how little we know, how often our judgments fall short and do not honor the wholeness of the other, settling in on things we dislike or disagree with or find irritating or obnoxious or not "up to our standards" however vaulted or arrogant those expectations may be.

We are loved into being. This is God's action, God's holy face. In turn, this is our action on behalf of the Holy One, to love one another into being, our own holy faces together with all the holy faces God has loved into being. Love is not a place at which one finally arrives, marked clearly as if a destination on the map of life. Neither is it a long stop along the way. *Loved into being* is a journey from birth to death. Watch a child respond to human affection and attention. Look into their eyes to find there the spark of their being, their spirit of life, their being as it connects with your own. Watch their bodies wriggle with the language of love, the powerful longing we all have to be loved, to belong. When you take a moment to be totally silent to consider all the people who have loved you into being, how does your body react? How does your spirit respond? Pay attention to a teenager with genuine affirmation, a personal compliment. All of us respond to expressions of love and affirmation because they affirm our presence in the world, our worth, our very existence. We truly are *loved into being.* Often our inclination to judge, make assumptions, or even diminish one another makes us incapable of loving others different from ourselves. We easily slip into self-absorption and self-justification as we assert our own wisdom, our own biases. No one is defined by one characteristic, one mistake or many of them, one "flaw." In our rush to define who we are and with whom we want to spend time, our measuring stick is often about who feeds our egos, who meets our needs, who affirms our ideas, our intellect, our personality type.

Long marriages require decades of development, shared notions of intimacy and steadfastness, fidelity and trust. Love is the foundation but it too is about being loved into being, over and over again. In a recent Emmy-award-winning television series, Ted Lasso is an American football coach invited to rescue a failing soccer team in the United Kingdom. He knows little about British soccer and is secretly expected to fail, thus fulfilling low expectations all around. But in each episode, Lasso's seemingly innate ability to invite cooperation over self-promotion, responsibility for others, respect, regard, and yes, love for one another slowly begins to turn the win-at-all-cost egos of athletes and their entangling alliances on their heads. They discover that the *we* is more important than the *I*, that winning is about mutuality and the common good. Compassion rears its beautiful face, anger begins to wear itself out, judgments are challenged, and a group of athletes and their friends begin to demonstrate integrity and unity, even genuine love for one another. It's a process and Lasso's gentle spirit of love is the backdrop, the foundation.

Many of us seem to have a propensity to judge, make assumptions, and generally default to critique as we interact with one another. Our own insecurities are often the depleted soil in which this happens. Everyone of us knows the sense of brokenness, the disappointment these qualities evoke. Our judgments are so often wrong and assumptions of ill will or negativity nearly always lead to dead ends. Why do we "go there" over and over again? When a room is infused with a spirit of grace, of love, of trust, our hearts are lifted up with gratitude and joy. Pleasure in another's company and the ability to embrace differences brings out the best in all of us. Faces literally shine from the light within as well as without—holy faces. Rather than tightly curling our fists or setting our jaws, perhaps we take the open hand of another human being reminding us—again—that we love each other into being.

> Love is patient, love is kind. It does not envy, it does not boast, it is not proud. It does not dishonor others, it is not self-seeking, it is not easily angered, it keeps no record of wrongs. Love does not delight in evil but rejoices with the truth. It always protects, always trusts, always hopes, always perseveres. Love never fails. (1 Cor 13:4–8)

Loved into being is a journey from birth to death. May each of our faces shine with love that empowers, that offers hope, that heals and restores life. Love is the greatest of gifts.

REFLECTION

We are loved into being—God's action and in turn, our action to love one another into being.

- Describe what happens when you *take one moment each day to be totally silent and consider all those people who have loved you into being?*
- In what ways is learning to love a lifelong challenge, hard work, a daily commitment—for you?
- Do you agree with the statement, "In our rush to define who we are and with whom we want to spend time, our measuring stick is often about who feeds our egos, who meets our needs, who affirms our ideas, our intellect, our personality type." Why or why not?
- First Corinthians 13 in the New Testament contains stunning words about the meaning of love. Read and reread these several verses and use them as an ongoing meditation.
- Christ embodies the cost of love in the Christian tradition. What might be the cost of love in your tradition?

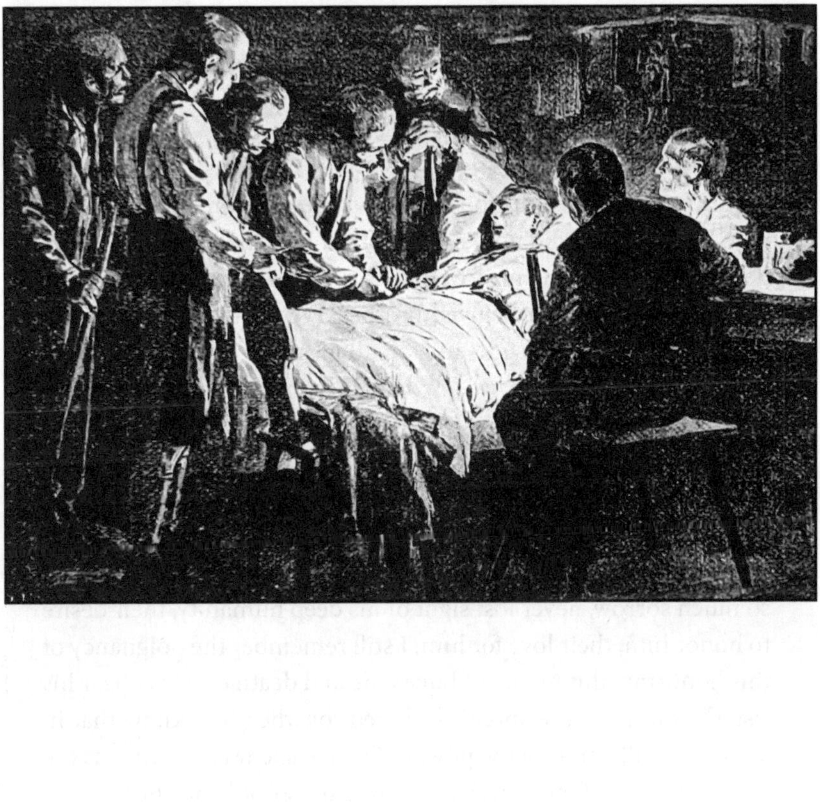

12

Luke

PERHAPS IT SEEMS ODD to focus this reflection on a man I never met. It's true that I did not know him, but Luke has occupied an indelible place in my memory despite this. It was his sister who shared the story of Luke, her beloved brother. We'd gathered with her, a Roman Catholic colleague, in a small group to talk about liturgy and the ways in which weekly rituals form us. Unsentimentally and clear-eyed, this obviously devoted sister began to tell us about Luke, his living and his dying. She wanted us to know him, the person he was, what his life was like. It wasn't pretty. Her matter-of-fact words and images told volumes about a man whose life was broken in many ways and of a family who, in spite of or because of so much sorrow, never lost sight of his deep humanity, their desire to honor him, their love for him. I still remember the poignancy of this honoring, this telling of Luke's life and death even as I hear his sister's voice, feel the space we shared together, and know that in addition to illustrating the power of ritual, she was showing us the face of the Holy One as well as the face of her holy brother.

Luke lived on his family's small farm in northern Minnesota. He'd never married and perhaps it was a relief for his siblings, now grown and gone, that he tried to maintain some semblance, however bleak it may have been, of the family's identity and livelihood among the rolling hills of Minnesota lake country. That worked for the first years of his adult life. But when the weight of the world or the farm or his own particular demons grew too heavy, Luke found solace in alcohol. In spite of the beauty and responsibility of his surroundings, the love of his siblings, and his deep roots in Catholicism, alcohol offered him escape and perhaps comfort. And when the demands for escape and comfort began to haunt his life on a daily basis, the disease of alcoholism came to dominate every aspect of his life. Soon the run-down farm became the palette against which his fragmented life spiraled out of control. If it once had been a warm and welcoming home for him and for his siblings, it now was part of a sorrow he could not bear. The pain of Luke's life ended early in his middle age, at his own hand.

His brokenhearted family, likely consumed by grief and their own guilt and sadness at not having been able to help Luke, gathered to mourn and to prepare his body for burial. These are the images that made an unerasable mark on me so many years ago. The siblings came together in the house where Luke had lived and where each of them had grown up. With deep emotion and reverence, they surrounded Luke with their presence, their tear-stained faces, their hands, rough and smooth, gentle and halting. They washed his body, praying words of forgiveness and unfailing love over him. They marked his brow with a cross of oil, and then dressed Luke in clean clothing. I imagined it to be white, like the baptismal gown he'd worn as a newborn, like the pall that would soon cover his coffin signifying new life in Christ and the dignity of Luke's life no matter how broken it may have been.

Following a wake and the gathering of more family and friends—Luke's body now placed in a wooden coffin, the church prepared for his funeral. And sometime while all those preparations were taking place, this happened. Luke's siblings found a tall ladder in the old barn that sat alongside a busy county road at the edge of the family's farm. One of them brought a gallon of paint and brushes and the bravest of the sisters and brothers took turns climbing that long ladder to paint Luke's name in giant letters across the entire face of the old barn—*his name was*

LUKE. In this act of holy remembering, Luke's siblings honored their much-loved brother. In this act of holy remembering, God welcomed Luke into the embrace of the community of saints, all of them broken in ways too numerous to count. In this act, Luke's siblings recognized his holy face and celebrated his holy life.

I've never forgotten Luke nor did I *ever* meet him. But I do know him. We all know the troubled "Lukes" who have graced our lives for good or ill. Indeed *all of us* are marked with broken dreams, disappointments, things we'd rather keep to ourselves—we all carry so much baggage. With Luke's siblings, I honor his life and the pathos of his death. I will not forget the tender voice of his sister as she told us, a group of strangers, the poignant story of her beloved Luke. Neither will I forget the loving hands and the holy presence of those sisters and brothers who prepared his body to be buried and painted his name for all the world to see. Rest in peace, dear Luke. And may all the other Lukes of our lives be honored and granted so fine a farewell.

REFLECTION

His name was LUKE.

- What images of Luke's life strike you as particularly poignant?
- If you could speak with Luke's siblings, what would you ask them?
- What does it mean to understand Luke's face as holy? Our own Luke's faces as holy? The face of God?
- What other holy faces might you find here?

13

Make of yourself a light . . .

Today as the soft light of morning rises slowly over snow-topped mountains in the distance, clouds scatter suddenly and the brilliance of the sun breaks through to cast light and warmth across a colorful quilt on my bed. Waking earlier with images from the evening news still fresh in my mind, my heart is heavy. War is raging in our world again and the weight of anguish grows exponentially as each dreaded day passes into the next. The chaos and sheer horror of such egregious attacks on innocent people and their beautiful land have sent the world reeling. A bit later I stop to notice those same rays of morning light now glimmering in perfect symmetry across hardwood floors. In the quiet of that moment I step into the pattern of light—so predictable and dependable—to let it wash over my feet. My body relaxes and my mind calms. The worry and fear have not gone away and I cannot and must not shake their presence. But the promise and hope of a new day shining its light across my bed and along the floor beneath my feet will have the last word.

Three holy faces also have their way with my anxious soul this day. Quaker writer and poet, Parker J. Palmer, has shared once again his heartfelt and humane wisdom on social media. As he often does, Palmer borrows broadly from others who inspire him casting a wide net that includes writer, Mary Oliver. She in turn begins her poignant poem, "The Buddha's Last Instruction," with an image of the Buddha himself.[1] The words of all three wash over me and I join my voice, my light, my holy face to theirs. We are borrowing from one another to keep our fears at bay and the demons they induce at arm's length.[2]

Oliver, waking herself to the rising sun of each new day, begins by quoting the dying Buddha. "Make of yourself a light," said the Buddha before he died, she writes. Oliver then paints a picture of the Buddha as he lay in the last moments of his life in the shade of two sala trees speaking to a sea of frightened faces looking to him for comfort. Oliver acknowledges the import of the moment saying something akin to "surely he had all kinds of wisdom to impart but these are the five words he chose."[3] And to underscore the insight they convey, Oliver returns to the theme of light, turning herself toward the rays of morning sun where she finds the transforming wonder of light and her own inexplicable worth and value.

The Buddha's was a last offering to the frightened villagers gathered at his feet. Oliver makes of it her own offering, acknowledging that she too wakes to morning light and that no matter the weight of worry she carries, that light empowers her to claim her own authority, her own voice and holy face, her own agency to *be* light herself. And without any reminding, Parker J. Palmer tells us that *we* are the frightened crowd before the dying Buddha, we are the horrified masses watching the terrors of war, and that there are many ways to make light, that light comes in a variety of forms:

- light that allows us to find our way home in the dark
- the light of human kindness that comforts everything it touches
- truth-telling that sheds light on outrageous and toxic lies

1. Palmer, "In Times of Deep Darkness."

2. With gratitude and appreciation for Parker J. Palmer, Mary Oliver, and the Buddha.

3. Oliver, "Buddha's Last Instruction," 4.

- light that illumines pathways toward a better world
- light that gives us courage to walk those pathways[4]

In these dark days where we see daily accounts of innocent people fleeing for their lives, the terrified faces of children mirroring the nightmare that surrounds them, it takes fortitude and resolute bravery to face such evil and act against it. Longing for calm, we know we must hold ourselves accountable for the atrocities happening before our eyes; but we cannot maintain balance or usefulness without keeping our eyes on the light, without *being* the light we seek. And so we dig more deeply to hold our fears and our grief side by side with confidence and courage. We shine light that allows us and others to find our way home in the dark. We share the light and comfort of human kindness. We pay attention to propaganda and refute toxic lies. With unfailing hope and gritty courage, we help illuminate pathways toward a better world. With confidence and determination, we find the power of our own voices to claim the light we seek. And as we do these things, we walk with those caught in the living hell and darkness of war, becoming the light the world needs so desperately.

Pay attention to the beauty and goodness of life. But do not turn away from the horror of burning buildings and bodies and the pictures of fleeing refugees. Lift your face to the sun and let raindrops wash away your tears. But open your heart to the mother giving birth on a gurney as she's carried from the ruins of a collapsing hospital and to the patients in another hospital being used as human shields. Listen to the voice of a pope whose own tears flow freely, who never fails to make of himself a light. But do not hesitate to condemn the words of those who distort truth and tell disgraceful lies. Tell the stories of heroism and bravery, of people willing to defend liberty by living and dying for one another. But do not shrink from naming and denouncing the forces of evil. Make of your home and heart a refuge, a place where God dwells, a place of welcome. As the madness of war haunts our waking and our sleeping, let us join our hearts and voices—our own

4. Palmer, "Make of Yourself a Light."

holy faces—with millions of others to spread light and to *be* light. "Make of yourself a light," said the Buddha before he died. Light will have the last word.

REFLECTION

In these dark days where we see daily accounts of innocent people fleeing for their lives, it takes steely fortitude and resolute bravery to face such evil and act against it. "Make of yourself a light," said the Buddha. Light will have the last word.

- Discuss some ways you find light in the darkness.
- What does it mean to "be the light you seek?"
- How does truth-telling become light? Hope?
- What does it mean to you to find your way home in the dark? What is the light that allows you to do this?

14

Making Good Trouble

The deeply lined face and determined presence of John Lewis, former member of the House of Representatives from the state of Georgia, will be engraved for decades in the annals of American history and in the memories of thousands—perhaps millions—of Americans who recognized a prophet in their midst. But it was the resonant voice and unwavering passion of a resolute John Lewis that still ring in our ears and echo in our hearts. "Make good trouble!" he exhorted, his voice booming and his charge clear. The stories are legend, the suffering excruciating, the spirit of this man unforgettable—from his childhood in rural Alabama to his heroism in the Civil Rights Movement and all the way to the halls of Congress and his death in 2020. We owe a great debt to this selfless servant whose life reflected extraordinary resilience, clear-eyed realism, and undeterred hope. These days many of us still long for his single-minded and unrelenting call to justice, his holy face and preacher's gifts of courage and empowerment.

John Lewis, a son of Alabama sharecroppers, spent his childhood working side by side with his parents and nine siblings chafing even then at the injustices of segregation. As a young boy, his interaction with white people was minimal; even so, he was clearly aware of the widespread inequities of the Jim Crow South. Worried for his safety, his parents discouraged his activism asking him to tread more slowly and act more cautiously. But Lewis was observant and when Rosa Parks and then Martin Luther King became household names, he found their courage and nonviolent resistance to segregation compelling and convicting. He met both Parks and King when he was a student seeking to desegregate a southern college that had refused to admit him. He'd always been a good student, an avid reader and learner, and now his parents encouraged him to use his gifts of leadership and speaking to become an ordained minister. He graduated from the American Baptist Theological Seminary and was then admitted to Fisk University, graduating with a bachelor's degree in religion and philosophy.

But the siren call of the Civil Rights Movement and the inspiration of its leaders captivated him. Soon John Lewis was joining nonviolent sit-ins and demonstrations, meeting with activists who shared his driving passion for freedom and equal rights. He was first arrested during the early Freedom Rides when with twelve other civil rights leaders he rode interstate buses to protest the law prohibiting black and white passengers from sitting together. He was elected to leadership roles in multiple civil rights organizations and helped organize the March on Washington in 1963. When Republican George Wallace, a radical segregationist governor of Alabama, ordered protesters to be beaten and whipped in the peaceful march from Selma to Montgomery a year later, Lewis and many others were attacked savagely by state troopers and police wielding bull whips and billy clubs. The fact that it was televised in millions of American homes made that march one of the most defining moments of the Civil Rights Movement. Those who witnessed the hatred and brutal violence of racism that Bloody Sunday would be impelled to support countless protests and demonstrations, finally resulting in the Voting Rights Act giving Black Americans the right to vote. Lewis had suffered a fractured skull, the first of many fractures and brutal physical attacks, and he nearly died. The scars he bore for the rest of his life were both physical and mental. John Lewis knew that the cornerstone of democracy is the right to vote and that unwavering conviction became the hallmark issue for him. John Lewis was "making good trouble."

Now several years after his death, John Lewis's legacy of "making good trouble" continues to ring in my ears. His gifts of courageous, compassionate servant leadership were evident in the ways he treated ordinary people—his brothers and sisters of every race, strangers on the street, his family, his constituents and his staff, as well as those in high places. He lived what he believed. His prophetic voice echoed the prophets he'd studied as a seminary student. He knew the evils of discrimination and he was an unrelenting witness to radical faith and justice for all. He also was at peace with himself, grounded and resolute. His hopefulness belied the agonizing journey for equal rights in the United States that continues to be a rallying cry for what most Americans know to be right and good. But Lewis did not give up. His dogged pursuit of justice was legendary and his spirit irrepressible.

What does it mean to "make good trouble?" John Lewis took his early training from Martin Luther King Jr., listening to the soaring oratory of another Southern preacher whose passion for justice helped shape young Lewis. Grounded in lifelong religious commitments, Lewis is said to have practiced his own oratory skills "preaching" as a boy to the chickens on his family's farm. Those religious commitments helped shape a keenly honed moral compass and single-minded focus tempered by authentic love and compassion. He would not tolerate the subjugation of his people or any other marginalized peoples. He practiced what he preached. Together with others who've given their lives to freedom and justice for all, Lewis was committed to nonviolence and found his true calling literally in laying down his life for others. For him, this was making good trouble.

John Lewis spent his life propelled by his religious identity and compelled to act politically and personally. He embodied the best of servant leadership and his words and selflessness continue to inspire and motivate.

> You are a light. You are the light. Never let anyone—any person or any force—dampen, dim or diminish your

> light. Study the path of others. . . . Lean toward the whispers of your own heart, discover the universal truth, and follow its dictates. . . . Release the need to hate, to harbor division, and the enticement of revenge. Release all bitterness. Hold only love, only peace in your heart, knowing that the battle of good to overcome evil is already won. Choose confrontation wisely, but when it is your time don't be afraid to stand up, speak up, and speak out against injustice. And if you follow your truth down the road to peace and the affirmation of love, if you shine like a beacon for all to see, then the poetry of all the great dreamers and philosophers is yours to manifest in a nation, a world community, and a Beloved Community that is finally at peace with itself.[1]

We know how much there is to be done and we know we are called to look at the world with eyes and hearts wide open, *to be the light*—listening, acting, watching, reading. John Lewis brought the searing experiences of discrimination and racial injustice to his life and to his work. May we too find the courage to speak and act on behalf of others, to open our hearts and lay down our own lives with humility and generous grace as together we make good trouble.

REFLECTION

The siren call of the Civil Rights Movement and the inspiration of its leaders captivated John Lewis. Now several years after his death, John Lewis's legacy of "making good trouble" continues to ring in my ears.

- John Lewis said, "Choose confrontation wisely, but when it is your time don't be afraid to stand up, speak up, and speak out against injustice." What empowers you to speak and act, to confront? What keeps us from these things?

1. Lewis, *Across That Bridge*, 177–78.

- The agonizing journey for justice and civil rights in this country continues. What do you think it will take finally to end widespread discrimination and racial injustice?
- What might it mean to *follow your truth down the road to peace and the affirmation of love* or *to shine like a beacon for all to see?*
- Name some ways that "making good trouble" brings justice and peace. What is the cost?

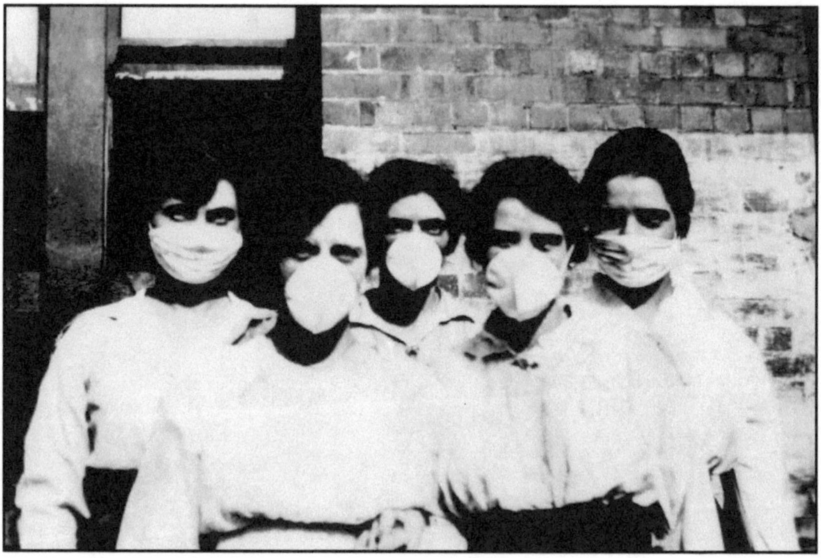

15

Pandemic Faces

When word came early in the winter that a vicious virus was making the rounds in Asia, we could not know (and perhaps it was *better* we could not know) that in just a matter of months, thousands and then millions of people would die. It still seemed remote, far away, and not terribly threatening. We knew something of its origins and expected we'd know how to deal with it if indeed it became a reality on our continent. But sooner than anyone expected, cases began to be reported outside of Asia, and when the ever-present news cycles began showing footage from inside hospitals in Italy and in a matter of days reporting hundreds of deaths and sharing photos of stacked caskets lined up outside churches and cemeteries waiting for burial, the reality of a pandemic became shockingly clear.

Among my earliest memories in those confusing first months of 2020 was the poignant appearance of Andrea Bocelli in the Milan Duomo on Easter Sunday. The cavernous cathedral was empty, the streets of Milan deserted. Around the world, most churches and cathedrals accustomed to celebrating the great Feast of the Resurrection were closed, silent. But on that sorrowful Easter Sunday in northern Italy where deaths from COVID-19 were exploding exponentially every day, Andrea Bocelli's unforgettable tenor voice reverberated around the world. Without comment, he sang "Panis Angelicus," the "Ave Maria," and "Domine Deus" before walking outside to perform "Amazing Grace" from the steps of the largest cathedral in Italy. Bocelli sang of resurrection and new life, his soulful presence and resilient faith haunting and extraordinary reminders of hope in the face of so much death. Many of us will never forget the radiant face and unforgettable voice of the blind artist from Tuscany as he offered a collective prayer on behalf of the world that dark Easter Sunday in Milan.

Faces of families from Italy affected by COVID-19 dominated the news, soon followed by the rest of Europe. And very quickly, the pandemic known as novel coronavirus spread to every continent, a veritable siege made all the more virulent by the rapid spread of information and the fear it generated. In the United States, the first cases to be reported happened on the West Coast at a home for the elderly in Seattle. And in a matter of days, the news channels were showing pictures of heartbroken families, their loved ones isolated in hospitals or makeshift medical units set up when hospitals could no longer provide space for the growing numbers of infected people.

The first person to be diagnosed in our state was a healthy man in his thirties who worked in the elementary school where our grandson was a first-grader. As the community went into high alert and our own family self-quarantined, the coronavirus suddenly became an alarming omnipresence. No longer could we hold it at arm's length. We were worried about our little one and all the children with whom this lovely school custodian interacted every day. We were worried about him, now in intensive care and close to death, and his family. No longer could we go to one another's homes, shop for groceries, or gather in public places without fear of infection. With so much of the world, we isolated ourselves from family, friends, and our normal patterns of daily life, hunkering down to protect ourselves and everyone around us.

And so the long, seemingly endless sea of faces began, many known to us and thousands unknown. At first, there were the solemn faces of medical professionals transporting white body bags from the retirement home in Seattle. I remember a photograph of the lead nurse in that care center, her eyes heavy with fatigue and worry. Later we learned that earlier cases were appearing on the East Coast. Then the evening news moved to what became a massive outbreak in New York City where outside many of the city's hospitals, caskets were again stacked high waiting for burial. The faces of masked doctors and nurses were everywhere, many of them being interviewed or recording physically and mentally exhausting days from their cars after work before driving home—often to care for children now doing school virtually or for elderly parents or other family members. Those shell-shocked faces, bone-weary and brokenhearted, are etched into my memory bank. Nightmare is not hyperbole for the bedlam and fear much of the world was feeling but there was no waking and it was no dream.

And as the world waited for answers, we watched the daily numbers of victims rise steadily, aggressively, now more than a million dead in the United States and almost five million globally. One in every four COVID deaths leaves a child without their parent or a primary caregiver. The faces of epidemiologists, scientists, and medical experts doing their level best to keep the public informed show exhausted fatigue and sometimes anger when efforts to stop the wildfire spread of disease are undermined by ill-informed political leaders and their sympathizers who continue to challenge medicine and science, turning a global crisis into a political game. The harsh realities of a pandemic became even more confusing with constant misinformation and mindlessly divisive chatter, treachery that contributes to so much needless death.

As effective vaccines have been identified and made available, a new line of defense brings much needed relief. But in their wake, new viral strains appear calling for additional research, different vaccines. Public and private schools, colleges and universities that had only recently reopened, have had to go back to the drawing board to determine how best to protect students and faculty. The economic toll on businesses and services continues. Churches, mosques, and synagogues have had to reshape and reformat their modes of gathering. To isolate, millions of Americans and others around the world have exchanged office spaces for workplaces at home. Others who work in the service industries remain in harm's way, hoping against hope not to "get it." Restaurants, theaters, sporting events, and more continue to adapt, adopting new ways to protect patrons—all of this confusing and chaotic, an eerie reminder of a world in turmoil.

Behind the masked faces, young and old and everyone in between, on the faces hidden by respirators and surgical coverings, in the tear-stained faces pressed against windows aching to touch and be touched by those on the other side—behind *all* the faces filled with unbearable grief and fear and loneliness, we watch and tremble at the ongoing and unrelenting grief wreaked by a pandemic. So much suffering. So much tragic loss. So much death. And so with gratitude for science and vaccines, for medical expertise and mutual hope for the common good, we look hopefully to the day when we can look back on this nightmare from enough distance to be reflective. We know our fragility is part of the human condition. We know we are not invulnerable. Perhaps the biggest lesson for us is the importance of caring for one another, depending on one another, supporting and protecting one another—from a cathedral in Milan to home offices and cubicles to hospital rooms and classrooms, spaces where the human spirit can continue to soar like the magnificent voice of Bocelli, his soulful presence and resilient faith hauntingly extraordinary reminders of hope in the face of so much death.

REFLECTION

Behind the masked faces, all the faces masking fear and grief and loneliness, we watch the ongoing havoc wreaked by a pandemic.

- Go to YouTube or Spotify to listen to *Music for Hope: Live from the Duomo di Milano*
- Describe your first experiences of the COVID pandemic.

- Which faces are etched in your memory? Why are they so unforgettable?
- What gives you hope? Resilience?

16

Prodigal and Beloved

THIS STORY, SO FRAUGHT with emotion, is hard for me to share. Like the biblical parable of the prodigal son, it is filled with despair. Unlike the story of the prodigal son, it does not end well. There was no homecoming feast and it continues to haunt us all, a virtual well of darkness. For many months and several years, I have tried to make sense of what I cannot understand, aching to know ways to alleviate a pervasive sense of loss, betrayal, and not-so-hidden hopelessness. It isn't that we expect to find peace, my family and I. And there are no illusions about our ability and our inability to honor this little brother of ours, this father of three remarkable young women, this friend of so many, this brother who at the age of sixty-two took his own life. The act itself haunts us all. There is no coming back from suicide. His loving letter of explanation and farewell while hollow in some ways, still echoes in our hearts. His daughters and my sisters and I will struggle the rest of our lives to understand and accept such senseless loss. In a last act of desperation, he wrote to us about a life without joy, empty and hopeless, without any reason for living. How does one find peace in a life empty of joy?

Describing what he meant to us in life is confusing enough. Describing what his death means apart from our stunning loss is complicated and in no way adequate or definitive. Every day is different. Every dream is confused with his being there but not there. Did we really know him? I do not know. But I want to honor my brother—Martin, Marty, Mart, Mungie—because he was our brother, the father of three beautiful nieces, a patriarch charged with ongoing patriarchy passed down generation to generation, an only son for whom expectations were high, heavy, and perhaps confusing and misplaced. He was a child of loving parents and a loving family who in spite of it all, could not find peace. He was a rascal, funny and irrepressible, often pushing boundaries and challenging authority. Island life is isolating and it was clear that the depth of his loneliness was only exacerbated during the long days and endless months of a pandemic. He was complicated, as most of us are, but to have ended his life as he did leaves each of us speechless and broken in our own ways.

He took sole responsibility for his tragic death in the hope, we are sure, that none of us would bear guilt or embarrassment or the heavy weight of such an act. If comfort was his expectation, he failed miserably. At a memorial service following Marty's death, we honored his memory and conveyed his wish that we speak on his behalf about a loving God who welcomes us all but, most especially, a God who welcomes the broken and the lost, a holy presence incapable of abandoning *any* of us. I suspect he felt himself to be both broken and lost and yet he knew a God of grace, forgiveness, and love. He was a devoted father, a good and loyal friend, a fine writer, and an avid lover of boats and fishing and island life. He was also a defrocked pastor, finally pushing boundaries to their limit and bringing hurt and humiliation to himself and too many others. How does one process such contradictory characteristics?

I hear his voice, his laughter, his seeming lightheartedness. I see his squint-y eyes so filled with light and the pleasure of being with people he loved. I feel his tenderness in the ways he cared for his daughters, helping them grow up as preacher's kids, supporting their interests in sports and in health care, in human rights and politics. They remember him as a storyteller, savoring his long narratives about made-up people and places, treasuring nightly adventures to lands near and far, sharing the unforgettable pleasures of reading together. They remember shared fishing trips and forays around Puget Sound, river rafting and camping excursions. He was a fabulous cook who made school lunches for his daughters and he could make a feast with a fish and a few fresh vegetables or grill a slab of beef fit for royalty. He loved to hunt, often serving venison cooked to perfection. His love of boats and the sea were life-giving but not enough to satisfy him professionally. And somewhere along the journey of his life, he lost his way. The moorings that had served him in earlier years seemed to have gone missing. Separation and divorce were sorrows he did not want.

Mart's countenance, his face and his presence in our lives, are carried with so much confusion. He was the little brother my sisters and I adored, the son our parents welcomed with great joy. He delighted in his daughters, proud of and humbled by their intelligence, their accomplishments. He was full of life, adventurous, daring. His friends were loyal and lifelong. He was also somehow broken and in search of something he could never find. He did not share feelings easily or open himself to those closest to him. He bore some notions of masculinity and entitlement that his daughters and sisters found offensive or at best misguided and sometimes inappropriate. We are painfully aware of the hurt he caused, both to the church and to his family, and to those whose lives are likely affected forever. Still, his love for his daughters and his family was authentic and genuine. He took great pleasure in his dogs, training them and teaching them to hunt. He loved his black lab, Moxie, and grieved her death until he himself died.

There seem to be few life lessons here, only deeply felt sorrow for a life now lost to us compounded by the sorrow of all we do not understand or comprehend. The one measure of peace to be found is the vision of our brother, prodigal and beloved, being enveloped in the loving arms of a gracious-beyond-our-wildest-imaginings God. If you know the biblical parable, you'll recall a father who, upon seeing his miserably hapless son off in the distance, kicks off his own sandals, hikes up his robes, and literally races with joy to embrace this lost one and welcome him home. That our brother knew the constancy of a loving God even in the midst of his own brokenness brings solace and consolation.

My desire to share my brother's story comes from a longing to make sense of a holy life and, yes, a holy face I knew only in part. We often do not know the hidden demons or the complicated issues of another's life. Perhaps it seems easier to conceal things we aren't comfortable sharing, things we may not even understand or comprehend ourselves. For me, that seems especially true of this beloved brother of mine. Without ignoring the dark side and without enhancing my brother's best characteristics, I want to celebrate his life even as we continue to grieve his sorrowful death. Prodigal and beloved. Life-giving and life-destroying. I will miss him forever.

REFLECTION

My need to share this story comes from a longing to make sense of a holy life and yes, a holy face I knew only in part. Prodigal and beloved. Life-giving and life-destroying.

- What words of comfort would *you* offer a family grieving a complicated life, a complicated death?
- Do you see hidden life lessons that seem to be unseeable to us? What might they be?
- What do you make of my brother's desire to share words of a loving and gracious God, a holy presence who embraces the broken and the outcast, the lost?
- Read or reread the parable of the prodigal son (Luke 11:15–32).

17

Sabbath Faces

For most of us, daily life is an ever-changing panoply of joys and sorrows, what sometimes may feel like a roller coaster ride as we plummet between peaks and valleys and the quieter, calmer spaces in between. Twenty-first-century life is complex just as life has always been. But our search for peace and contentment may be more complicated. Where do you find hope when hopelessness comes knocking at your door? How do you manage to balance the complexities of life that challenge the most irenic of spirits? How do you and how does your community keep equilibrium? None of us is able to find hope and peace alone in what too often seems a despairingly broken and violent world.

This has been another dark week, the pictures of a massacre in an elementary school emblazoned across our screens, voices of parents and teachers and law enforcement officers describing the indescribable, our hearts and souls broken again by such horror. Only days earlier we grieved a racially motivated supermarket shooting in another corner of this country, taking the lives of more innocent people as they shopped for groceries. This ongoing rampage is rampant in a country bent on allowing free access to weapons of destruction. "Where are you, God? Where were *you* when the last mass shooter took the lives of nearly two dozen people, most of them six, seven, and eight-year olds?" "I keep waiting for you to show up, dear God; to protect and comfort, to assure and hold accountable, to make sense of such horror—where *are* you, God?" But the lens of horrific events is wider than this week's news. It includes graphic pictures of a shockingly immoral war in Ukraine. It shows haunting faces of people struggling to buy food and gasoline and tells frightening stories of corruption and political misconduct. The world seems out of control.

Yes, I listen to the echoes of bird song nearly every morning and find the beauty of spring irresistible as we plant bare-root lupine in the damp earth—life-balancing prayer for me. The hummingbirds are back, flitting among the flower pots filled with blossoming masses of colorful annuals, taking their fill of life-giving nectar—signs of resilience, symbols of hope. A pileated woodpecker has wakened us again today with its insufferable attacks on a metal chimney outside our window. The tides continue to ebb and flow and I see new life has joined the whale pod swimming the saltwater channel near my childhood home in Puget Sound. Why can't nature's celebration of spring and resurrection translate into the dark human spaces where fear and hate and greed seem to propagate like tenacious weeds? I am looking for signs of resurrection, rebirth, and reawakening!

Still, I am surprised every week by a tangible yet extraordinary experience of God's life-giving presence in the middle of such darkness—God's face among the ordinary faces of Sabbath. There, in that space where I worship surrounded by a world of hurt and brokenness, is a body of people no more immune from suffering and deep hurt than anyone else on this planet. They are old and young, hardy and frail, teachers and students, grocery store clerks and innocent shoppers—all survivors of another difficult week. But in that Sunday morning ritual and in spite of the chaos all around us, we look one another in the eye to offer peace and forgiveness, love and grace, sympathy and joy, grief and hope—life-giving gestures and compelling signs of resurrection and new life.

In my tradition, there is a table in that place where all are welcomed and fed; the littlest children walk confidently ahead of parents to receive a broken bite of bread, the body of Christ, a tiny cup of wine or grape juice, the blood of Christ. Old people shuffle their way forward; several come in wheelchairs or carry canes. There are newly widowed people, their grief visibly present; several carry the weight of life-threatening health issues. With their eyes fixed on the bread and the wine, young and old and everyone in between seems to recognize in these signs life-saving hope. This happens *every* week. And hope never gets old.

There is a time and place for reading the holy texts; from this spot, ordinary people take turns proclaiming the weekly readings, stories of ancient people also seeking peace and meaning in the chaos of life. Having studied the texts and participated in the events of another challenging week, a pastor or priest leads the community into the weekly readings. When that pastor or priest wrestles honestly with the stories of Scripture together with the events of people's lives and news from around the world, listeners are invited to their own honest wrestling, their own questions and worries and uncertainties. Authenticity, truth-telling, and question-making are powerful bearers of hope. They empower and enable action. And they signify the presence of potent and holy things. Words matter. Ritual matters. We matter. The world matters.

In my tradition, there is a place for lighting candles to remember or grieve or celebrate; there is a font of water in which to dip one's fingers to make the sign of the cross or simply to feel its fluidity and be reminded that water is the source of life. These ordinary experiences on a Sabbath morning have extraordinary power. The welcome is heartfelt, warm, a quiet summoning of God's presence and power among worshipers, acknowledging the hurts of the world and of our own lives. Without being trite or entitled or commonplace, there is a palpable sense of hallowed ground and holy presence. There is music and liturgy, words chanted and words sung in response—plaintive and longing, upbeat and hopeful, rhythmic and sometimes playful. Occasionally there are tears and sometimes there is laughter.

I have participated in this Sabbath ritual all my life. It has not always been edifying and on occasion I have come away feeling oddly empty, longing for some concrete sense of the holy, frustrated with worn platitudes or pious language no longer compelling. When the rituals of worship seem to echo a sporting event or a rally of one kind or another, I am left wanting and longing for tangible evidence of something deeper, more lasting and dependable. I am waiting to encounter the Holy One in each other and in the world. But most Sabbath mornings there are faces, gestures, images, and words that convey resurrection and new life. These same faces are not restricted to Sundays only. There are heartfelt visits with family about illness and broken relationships. On Monday a tearful neighbor comes to apologize for her errant dog, telling me over and over again how sorry she is for his behavior and how she hopes to change it. There is hospitality shared with old friends and a satisfyingly rich phone conversation with someone struggling to make sense of life. Texts and notes detail daily lives that are fragile and fraught. We all carry heavy loads. But we also carry each other, helping one another bear the weight of grief and the burdens of life even as we treasure the gladness of life. These are sacramental encounters, every single one of them.

When these Sabbath faces, gestures, words and images are part of the weekly ritual, we are drawn into the mystery and presence of God in a world that overflows with suffering, violence, and injustice. We are nourished and empowered to embody God's immeasurable love and grace amid all the darkness and despair. In that Sunday morning ritual and its iterations during the week, we recognize God's presence in one another in spite of so much fear and despair. We offer each other hope, peace and forgiveness, love and grace, sympathy and joy—signs of resurrection and new life, signs of the Holy One.

"Where are you, God?" You are here, present in each of us and in *all* of creation, even as we groan and cry out in overwhelming darkness and even as we sing and celebrate the beauty and goodness of life.

REFLECTION

In that space where I worship surrounded by a world of hurt and brokenness, in that Sunday morning ritual, we offer one another peace and forgiveness, love and grace, sympathy and joy and hope—life-giving gestures and compelling signs of resurrection and new life.

- Where do you find life-saving, life-giving hope?
- What in your experience gives words and rituals the power to transform?
- Discuss some ways you find balance, equilibrium.
- How do you answer the question, "Where are you, God?"

18

Sentient dolphins and existential questions

THE WEEKLY GATHERING FOR teens and, by special invitation, a gaggle of mostly older adults in my parish, began with a question prompted by an image: on the computer screen in front of us was a friendly-looking dolphin leaping from the turquoise waters surrounding the sleek mammal. "Would you eat dolphin if you had the chance?" asked the teacher, a young man obviously gifted in his work with teenagers and young adults. No one said a word at first; it was hard to look at the face of that beautiful creature and consider whether or not one might eat it. But after a minute or so, a wise teenager in the front row spoke up. "No!" he said not so quietly, "it's a sentient mammal. I couldn't eat it." Then to make a point of the meaning of sentient, the teacher shared several more photos showing himself and his spouse swimming and playing with dolphins, humans and animals alike interacting and communicating with one another.

The class—a series called "The Kairos Hermeneutic"—was a thoughtful exploration about the complexities of interpreting the Bible. To begin the conversations, statements were shared from prominent conservative groups espousing and requiring adherence to a literal understanding of the Bible, a road map for life to be obeyed in full—word for word, truth with a capital T, the very voice and handwriting of God. These young people clearly had wrestled with this topic before and were quick with their "what ifs?" and "but that's wrong!" and "no way!" They were looking for authentic ways to make sense of biblical texts in their own twenty-first-century contexts—how to interpret dietary laws or arcane legal issues from a culture and time so different from our own. They found acts of war and violence unacceptable and narratives that subjugated women or ignored children offensive. Curious and not at all put off by subtle and not-so-subtle miracle stories, young and old alike agreed that the Bible can be baffling and bewildering for modern-day readers.

With honesty and learned expertise, the teacher helped illustrate ways in which biblical stories might inform twenty-first-century readers in our quest to understand and make sense of God's presence in this world. Their interest obviously piqued, the young students did not seem to be recipients of knowledge passed "down" but conversation partners and active players in an ongoing exploration of questions that matter. Using words like metaphor and nuance, ambiguity and uncertainty, words often not associated with religion and belief, these especially earnest, engaged teenagers and their adult companions exhibited curiosity and wisdom, wrestling together to make sense of a world that very often makes no sense, of a God that sometimes seems distant and unrelated to daily life, of a Bible not easily understood.

No one was interested in dismissing the importance of the holy book. There was nothing remotely flippant or glib about the Bible, its stories, the acts of God, or the ways it conveys God's love for all of creation. There was respect, even reverence, for the book which contains the stories of our Hebrew ancestors, tales of war and violence, the cries and laments of our forebears together with the stories of God's love and saving acts. But what I saw in those mask-covered faces those Sunday mornings during a worldwide pandemic was full-hearted willingness to question, probe, and grapple with questions of life and faith. "Would you eat dolphin if given the chance?" had to do with difficult choices, complicated issues, new understandings of the sacredness of life, the ability to recognize the connectedness of all created beings, and the nature of a mammal that feels and perceives and whose existence matters and is not somehow disposable or dispensable.

The striking faces of a talented teacher and his curious students juxtaposed with pictures of an affectionate dolphin and stories of faith that still have the power to form and inform our lives is a beautiful thing. When it happens that wisely inquisitive teenagers, empowered by their own confidence to engage in the ubiquitous dilemmas of knowing who we are and what God is like and how to make sense of existential questions is on full display, it's a beautiful thing. When a good teacher creates space where such exchanges are expected and embraced, lives are empowered and changed.

For askers of hard questions, young and old; for all who wrestle with doubt and uncertainty; for all who flourish when doors and windows are thrown open and questions are welcomed like rainwater in the desert, step right up! If you are put off by the complexities and inconsistencies of the Bible but know it to be life-giving and authoritative if not always right, listen to these voices willing to question and to learn. Be careful about proclaiming the Truth and generous to embrace ambiguity and uncertainty. Beware rigid notions etched in stone.

The Holy One cannot be neatly defined. The Holy Book is not to be worshiped. We are here to learn from it and *converse with it*, to probe the questions of the universe and the meaning of life together in our own time. I imagine a God who welcomes our uncertainties, perhaps bestowing an extra measure of grace on all who have the humility to know how little they know. Watching the wonder of dolphins at play with humans reminds me that all of life is holy and the holy Scriptures graphically illustrate the complexities. Watching a twenty-something teacher and learner who himself understands the Bible to be truthful and authoritative while acknowledging that it isn't always right and then opens doors and windows for his young (and old) charges to explore and question shows extraordinary grace and holy wisdom. Sentient dolphins, existential questions, and those striking faces—masked as they were, remind me that stories of faith, as confusing and difficult as they may be, have extraordinary power to form and inform. Those same conversations and their counterparts in every arena of faith and life help create thoughtfully reflective human beings who in turn continue to grow and learn and flourish in an often confusing world.

REFLECTION

The Holy One cannot be neatly defined. I imagine a God who welcomes our uncertainties and our wrestling with hard questions, including the complexities of holy texts.

- How do these issues address the sacredness of life and the ability to recognize the connectedness of all created beings?
- Name some ways you've grappled with hard questions and the complexities of Scripture.
- Do you agree that the Holy One cannot be neatly defined? Why or why not? That the Holy Book is not to be worshiped but conversed with? What might these conversations look like?
- What does the wonder of watching dolphins at play with humans evoke for you?

19

Sitting Shiva

Sometimes I envy my Jewish friends the rituals and prescribed practices that help them cope with life and death. In a culture especially eager to hide death and dying or to reduce it to a once-and-done funeral, the Jewish practice of sitting Shiva is a way of walking with and beside someone mourning the loss of a loved one following a funeral. Once the funeral has taken place, sitting Shiva begins: a time and a place for mourners to offer their presence, their support, their hearts to grieving family and friends. It's a time for consolation, comfort, solace. It's a way of entering into another's grief and loss, remembering and honoring the one who has died while attending to those left behind. Shiva usually lasts for seven days but can be shorter or longer depending on a family's needs. While all religious traditions and indeed many others who may not know a religious tradition practice some form of sitting Shiva, I find it a beautiful picture of the sanctity of life and our common need for one another. I want to think about sitting Shiva as a metaphor embodying our call to genuine friendship and caring presence—care for the earth, for the community and our neighborhood, and care for ourselves—God care. I want to think about the many ways we "sit Shiva" with one another.

It begins with mindfulness, with noticing one another and paying attention. That may mean noticing another's physical presence, listening to the nightly news, paying attention to the invisible ones who make sure we have running water, safe places to live, and food in our pantries. It may be seeing children who hide scars too deep for words or who lack security of one kind or another. It might mean that we withdraw from our normal routines and patterns of daily life to focus on a family of immigrants struggling to find their way in a new land, a foreign culture. Or it might be that we keep a list of people in need of a phone call or a text message or a card or letter, ways to communicate with and acknowledge one another. Often we share food, loaves of warm bread, a pot of soup, a sack of apples or a box of cookies. Sometimes, it's simply—and not so simply—sitting with someone, silently listening to their breathing and one's own quiet breath, holding a hand or sharing a cup of tea. I think of all these things as forms of prayer. We "do" Shiva in multitudes of ways.

Sitting Shiva may best be practiced without the boundaries of a funeral or a hospice space. How many times have we all wished we'd spent more time, paid better attention, listened more carefully? How many times have we forgotten that we need one another, in joy and in grief, in confusion and in certainty, in our darkest moments and in every moment in between. We do life better together.

Some years ago when South Africa was in the early throes of its long struggle against apartheid, the notion of Ubuntu found its way to the West. Desmond Tutu tells it like this: "Ubuntu is very difficult to render into a Western language. It speaks of the very essence of being human . . . my humanity is caught up, is inextricably bound up, in yours."[1] I understand it to mean that I am because we are, or that which humanizes others humanizes me, and conversely, that which dehumanizes others dehumanizes me. Ubuntu is a way of living in harmony. We sit Shiva with one another because that act of human care and compassion embodies our connectedness and what it means to belong to one

1. Tutu, *No Future without Forgiveness*, 31.

another. We sometimes forget this important lesson of life, our interdependence and our need to rely on one another both in good times and bad.

My sister recently sat Shiva by loading her car full of clothing belonging to a man who'd recently died. She promised his grieving spouse that she'd deliver it to their church's clothing closet, a place where street people can access free clothes. She is the same sister who regularly checks in on a woman and her two sons who are housebound and makes calls to another couple who rely on her for groceries and treats they cannot afford themselves. Another of my siblings shows hospitality to people from every walk of life, making and sharing meals over and over again, taking food to shelters and to shut-ins she may not even know. I remember my friend, Joan, once describing the people who begged outside the grocery store in our city. Without ever singling them out or debating with herself whether or not they were legitimately in need, or worse, tooting her own horn, she knew each of them as a holy face (in need or not), by recognizing their deep humanity and her responsibility to see it. I knew she never ever ignored a person on the street asking for money or food or some other handout. Joan sat Shiva most days in spite, no doubt, of being scammed again and again. How can one of us be happy if all the others are sad?

We are part of a world in desperate need of care. Showing up, engaging in conversation, being present, sharing silence, making food, showing generosity to strangers or kindness to someone barely hanging onto the edges of life is to sit Shiva. For years, a brother-in-law has helped students who've dropped out of school prepare to complete the high school graduate equivalency certificate (GED). For so many young people who've lost ground in ways too numerous to count, earning the GED opens the door to college, university, and trade school admissions. This same brother coaches and umpires junior high sports and participates in a community endeavor to provide housing for people without homes. We all know countless others who teach and educate, who govern and make laws, who provide healthcare, participate in community and church programs, offer day care for children and staff homes for the elderly, who keep our streets clean and our cities safe. This isn't to forget the faceless others who take the time in the middle of "ordinary" work and life to show kindness and interest in the people they meet. For that is what sitting Shiva is about: showing up, offering compassion and a generous spirit, grieving and celebrating, seeing every face as holy and deserving of our time and our care. I am because we are! How can one of us be happy if all the others are sad?

REFLECTION

Sitting Shiva is a way of walking with one another, of recognizing our shared humanity in joy and grief, in confusion and in certainty. How many times have we all wished we'd spent more time, paid better attention, listened more carefully? My humanity is bound up in yours.

- Have you had the opportunity to sit Shiva with a Jewish community? What was it like?
- Describe some ways you experience sitting Shiva in your tradition?
- How might care of the earth, the community, the neighborhood, and ourselves—God care, be a way of sitting Shiva? What does this mean for you?
- How is sitting Shiva a metaphor in your own life, for seeing every face as holy?

20

The holy faces of africa

I TELL THESE STORIES from memory filled with sights and sounds I hope never to forget. It was late February in East Africa and we'd arrived outside Arusha in Tanzania just days before. Our ten-year-old granddaughter was with us and we'd spent the first days getting acclimated and making contacts with old friends and new. From the beginning, Ingrid found the culture shock intoxicating. Wide-eyed and ready for adventure, her unabashed enthusiasm was matched by the small cadre of adults traveling with us. As we made our way in three well-worn Land Rovers on deeply rutted dirt roads into Arusha National Park and up into the tangled, jungle-like foothills of beautiful Mount Meru, our Tanzanian guide, Stephano, led the way.

"Elephants are rare here," Stephano told us, "but we'll likely see warthogs and water buffalo, giraffe, and several species of monkeys." And then as we bounced around a corner and out onto a wide and open plain, a family of elephants surprised us. One of them had climbed a tree and was perched between two very sturdy branches, astounding us at such a feat—yet we saw its nonchalant face with our own eyes. Our close-up introduction that day to the wild beauty of Africa was a foretaste of the feast to come. Ingrid was the first to spot a statuesque giraffe calmly watching us as we came around a corner, Ingrid's eyes as big as plates. Above us, black and white colobus monkeys leapt from treetop to treetop, the jungle air reverberating with their croaking voices as the Land Rovers below bounced and jolted between cavernous ruts and massive potholes and we humans craned our necks and held on for dear life. The jaw-dropping wonder of that day was only the beginning.

Part of our reason for being in Tanzania was to visit schools and healthcare sites, another set of experiences etched into my memory. The scrubbed faces of beautiful young children attending primary school lit up as we entered their environs, a set of rickety one-room huts surrounding a dirt playground. Their shining faces focused immediately on this blond-haired American child, just their age; and as children will, they rushed up to touch Ingrid's hair and her skin, grabbing her hands in a show of curiosity and affection. Listening later to the children's harmonious singing and then joining our voices to theirs was unforgettable—the joy and naturalness of it, the seeming spontaneity and sense of belonging to one another. We learned that day that most of those children walk many miles to a school where there is no lunch program, no drinking water, few books, and where school supplies are nonexistent except when brought by groups like ours and then divvied out like gold.

At a hospice for children needing surgeries for physical disabilities, a whole new experience awaited us. Parents and children waiting together for their turn in the surgical queue as well as those recovering from reconstructive surgeries greeted us from outdoor benches, wall-to-wall hospital beds in spare white cubicles, and in a schoolroom reserved for children well enough for occasional lessons. One young girl, Glory, had been at the hospice for more than a year after being badly burned when an iron pot for cooking over an open fire tipped over, falling onto her head and face and scarring her whole body. She'd begun a series of surgeries that would likely last another year or two. Her face, disfigured by fire and scar tissue, shone when we met her and called her by name. She held out her hand to Ingrid who knew instinctively to take it, scarred as it was. Children still healing from club foot surgeries played in the warm sunshine on that spring day, hobbling with help as they learned to walk again, many of them eager to be recognized and acknowledged. Inside the rooms, babies and toddlers still groggy from anesthesia or other medications were tended by medical staff. In the open-air courtyard at the center of the hospice, hopeful parents sat with children waiting their turn for a normal life. But in spite of the seriousness of life-changing deformities and the pain of daily life, the place seemed to sing with hope, so many faces filled with welcome for strangers, some eager to embrace a child from another land, joyful faces, holy faces.

Another day in the town of Monduli, we met a small throng of young women, girls from marginalized peoples like the Maasai, Barbaig, and Hadzabe tribes that understand teenage women mostly in terms of property to be sold. Because of primary teachers and others who recognize the importance of secondary education particularly for women, these spirited young girls who have shown unusual, even extraordinary academic promise have been chosen to leave their homes and tribes to study at a residential high school and then go on to earn degrees to become teachers, doctors and nurses, social workers and lawyers. To experience their determination and energy over being given such a chance to excel is unforgettably moving. Their journeys are mind-boggling and their resolve inspiring—for a ten-year-old American girl as well as her adult companions. To hear the girls' hopes and affirm their dreams was yet another glimpse of courage and promise. Their beautiful faces are engraved in my mind and I feel their arms wrapped around Ingrid and me and the others as they danced us across their school yard, proudly showing us the place that for them means a chance to explore the world and contribute to making it a better place for themselves and for their people. Ingrid's instinctive willingness to be embraced by them is caught in a photograph—their faces and hers lit up with joy—that hangs in a place of prominence in our home.

Each of these experiences demanded conversation and time for processing and interpretation. For the adults and for Ingrid, it was cultural overload. Holding her close as we bounced our way across random dirt paths in the Serengeti and down into Ngorongoro Crater, we tried to imagine life inside a cone-shaped Maasai boma or what it might be like to wear the hot, scratchy, traditional red-robed shawls worn by Maasai shepherds who dotted the vast countryside herding bony cattle and scrawny goats. And always, the constant sense of the vastness of Africa and all its beautiful creatures left us holding our breath, watching and waiting for what might appear around the next curve, below the next hill.

At Ndutu, the furthermost point in our explorations, I sat watching Ingrid as she wrote in her journal outside the small, thatched lodge overlooking a stretch of land teeming with wild creatures. The holy faces of Africa included her own beautiful face, seeing through her eyes and her young spirit so captivated by this land, its people, its animals. To be given such a glimpse of the world and to share it with others, especially with this beloved grandchild, is to recognize the beauty of all faces, to see holiness in creatures great and small, and to embrace people of every race and culture. Holy faces indeed!

REFLECTION

At Ndutu, I sat watching Ingrid as she wrote in her journal. The holy faces of Africa included her own beautiful presence, seeing through her eyes into her young spirit, so captivated by this land.

- The wild beauty of Eastern Africa is unforgettable. Describe a place or an experience you've had that still elicits wonder and awe.
- The faces described here include creatures both human and animal, as well as the face of the land itself. Why might that be important?
- What about this experience might leave a mark on you? What are its lessons?

21

The Human Library

GATHERING WITH OTHERS CAN be complicated and at best, it requires effort and making time. Many of us enjoy meeting new people, showing hospitality, and sharing conversation. Most of the time, we invite people we know or with whom we have common interests or find interesting; and reciprocity seems to take the same shape. We spend time with people familiar to us, those with whom we are comfortable. But what might it look like to seek out real conversations with those in our society who often are subjected to prejudice, being stigmatized or discriminated against in one way or another? It might be because of cultural differences or lifestyle choices. Too often it may reflect notions of social status or acceptance. It might be about a disability or a diagnosis that makes us uncomfortable. Often we are simply ill at ease with someone who looks or acts differently.

In 2000, something called The Human Library came into being in Denmark.[1] Using a library analogy of lending people rather than books, the Human Library was created to challenge stigma and stereotypes, paying attention to addressing people's prejudices by helping them talk to those they would not normally meet. By creating spaces where personal conversations between

1. Information in this chapter came from https://humanlibrary.org/.

human books and their reader could take place—literally a library of people where dialogue is safe and welcome, the Human Library was off and running.

In the information included on their website, this

> human library, or "Menneskebiblioteket" as it is called in Danish, was created in Copenhagen in the spring of 2000 by Ronni Abergel and his brother Dany and colleagues Asma Mouna and Christoffer Erichsen.
>
> The original event was open eight hours a day for four days straight and featured over fifty different titles [otherwise known as real-life people]. The broad selection of books provided readers with ample choice to challenge their stereotypes and so more than a thousand readers took advantage leaving books, librarians, organisers, and readers stunned at the reception and impact of the Human Library.[2]

When I first read about this phenomenon, now going strong with twenty-three-plus years of experience, I was blown away. How many times have we shied away from others because of our own discomfort with a mental health issue or cultural differences? How often have we viewed certain segments of society as inferior or lesser than (or worse, undesirable), making good people invisible? How many times do all of us default to judgmentalism, racism, classism, or any other of the isms that divide and hide us one from the other? Today these human libraries exist on six continents and they host or involve people in more than eighty countries. It isn't hard to imagine the impact they have for creating social change and breaking down barriers of difference and fear, ignorance and prejudice. Such an idea for seeing one another in all our beautiful diversity by creating safe spaces to converse shows deep humanity. Such a practice is a prime opportunity for seeing holy faces.

The human books are all volunteers who know their topic because of personal experience. They expect difficult questions and appreciate the chance to explain and interact with others genuinely interested in who they are and whatever human condition

2. Human Library, "About the Human Library," paras. 3–4.

or personal struggle they may know. Doors are opened for both the one who speaks and the one who listens, back and forth, creating a web of understanding and new ways of seeing each other. The human books include people with addictions, some who have done prison time, those who are bipolar, others who are without homes and living on the streets, and others who've made extreme changes to their bodies, using tattoos and piercings to modify how they look. Some are victims of sexual abuse. Immigrants and refugees tell stories of what it's like to leave one's homeland and how it feels to be an outsider. I imagine people with physical disabilities, who deal everyday with life in a wheelchair or who are singled out by the way they look. There are human books who are deaf and others who are blind. Without a doubt there are others who have discovered themselves to be lesbian or gay, bisexual or transgender, queer and/or questioning, and countless other ways in which people self-identify.[3]

The human family is large and we always are discovering one another. As a child, I remember a new book of photography called *The Family of Man*. It was endlessly fascinating to look at people from around the world, from cultures and climates and communities so different from my own. And in spite of the title which left out half the world's population, they did indeed include women and children and the beautiful faces of tribes and clans and families of all different configurations. It was a rich feast of diversity. An exhibit of the photographs opened at the Museum of Modern Art in New York City in the mid-fifties and then toured the world as a unique picture of humanity and human faces. The common themes were daily relationships: pictures of lovers and marriage and child-bearing; children of all ages; families struggling and celebrating and enduring the ups and downs of life; elders. Some pictures showed dreamers and faces filled with joy and hope; others were of people clearly suffering the pain of broken relationships and lives lived in hardship and conflict. Even as a little child, I could not put it down.

3. See https://humanlibrary.org/meet-our-human-books/

Our proclivity to default to judgment is a terrible thing, an evil that plagues the world. We fan the flames of fear and bias, even small-mindedness at our peril. To consciously seek to un-judge is a goal worthy of humans who do best in relationship with each other. In human libraries, it doesn't take long to understand that a human book is more than its cover, its face, and that relationships are always about helping us "open the book" to see and acknowledge another's holy face. When books are once again banned, most human beings stand up in protest, fearing the lies that destroy and tear down and undermine understanding and the ability to embrace difference. Perhaps the Human Library is a graphic picture of the human family in all its diversity and variety, a stunningly beautiful photograph of people made in the image of God, none of whom are banned.

Today the Human Library includes virtual events and actual gatherings in libraries and museums, in schools and universities, in churches, mosques and synagogues, at festivals and conferences. Human beings serving as open books is a clear call for understanding and acceptance. All of us know how desperately our world needs movements for social change, for truly seeing each other's faces and acknowledging all of humanity. In times as challenging as our own, may we each seek out the holy faces in the family of our shared humanity.

REFLECTION

The Human Library is a graphic project that does indeed celebrate the human family in all its diversity.

- Name some occasions when you've felt uncomfortable around people you didn't understand or know. Describe your feelings.
- What do you make of the first human library, open eight hours a day for four days straight and featuring over fifty different "titles," otherwise known as real-life people? The broad selection of "books" provided readers with ample choice to

challenge their stereotypes and more than a thousand readers took advantage leaving books, librarians, organizers and readers stunned at the reception and impact of the Human Library.

- Our tendency to default to judgment can be a terrible thing. Share examples of how it fans flames of fear and bias, even small-mindedness.
- Are there other ways to "open the book" and learn from those we may fear or with whom we feel uncomfortable. Name one or two.
- Would you participate in a human library? Why or why not?

22

Their shining faces

WHETHER WITH ME HERE at home or halfway around the world, the light of their shining faces is always with me. Still children, their passion for make-believe and "let's pretend" is contagious. Even when they were toddlers, they could transform a simple box into a mighty train wending its way across some distant continent where fierce animals and dark forests threatened at every bend in the winding road. As their worlds expanded, so did the adventures they'd create, especially when we were together and shared each other's undivided attention. Just last week we climbed a mountain to discover that Elsa had become a lost girl named Crimson while her brother, Holden, a photojournalist laser-focused on recording her every step, directed the drama from my elbow. Whispering not quietly from behind me, Holden would say, "Nana, Nana! Over this way, act more afraid, show that you're scared. Cry!" When they both were very little, we'd dance to music chosen by their mother, both of them snapping their fingers and swinging and swaying and bobbing as I tried to keep up. Later, they became Little Red Riding Hood and the gentle and doting grandmother who could turn on a dime into a big bad wolf. Sometimes the stories warped into varied versions of the Three Little Pigs or Goldilocks and the Three Bears.

The dramatic expressions on their shining faces are unforgettable. Oh, the places we've been!

I know this passion of theirs will be short-lived and I want to remember it for the rest of my days. Crimson, aka Elsa, may do a few more meanders around the mountain followed by her brother and doting grandmother. She'll be wearing a long flowing flowered dress, her jacket askew, too-big black boots that flop at every step, her long dark hair in a tangle, her eyes shining. Holden the filmmaker will have forgotten to turn on the camera so we'll begin again, not getting the lines quite right or to his liking. But he is patient and loves to draw out the play into as many acts as possible, all the better for hanging onto his powerful camera, Nana's magic iPhone. Trees become jungles and birds take on human proportions. A squirrel scurrying through the underbrush might be a flesh-eating savage or a poor lost child in need of care. And when a deer gracefully lopes across the meadow below us, we're caught between reality and make-believe, the three of us mesmerized by the elegance of this real-life creature. Grandpa suddenly appears on the trail below us, roaring up from the depths of the mountain, laughing at our zigzagging drama.

Back at home and still hankering to control the camera, they explain how to do slow-motion captures where their voices become deep and sluggish, drawn out in low tones and panoramic shots show them to be in two places at once, eyes shining and arms flailing. Holden becomes an interviewer asking hard questions of Grandpa who rises to the occasion, both of them seriously skilled at questioning and answering. When the kitchen becomes another set, we're suddenly cast as characters on a cooking show. Not to be outdone by Julia Child or the Great British Bake Off, we begin with an animated discussion about the food we plan to prepare. Exaggerated and dramatic, dressed in appropriate aprons equal to the job before us, Elsa chops onions while crying a stream of onion-induced tears that also fit the imagined "show." Holden steps up when the quesadilla-making gets more complex and Elsa becomes the producer and photographer. Red peppers and green become a colorful palate for a uniquely homemade cooking show.

In between shoots, much sampling takes place and the floor below becomes a catch-all matching the mess on the counter above.

These are children whose lives have been influenced by Xbox and PlayStation, Nintendo and the magic of Harry Potter. In an interactive game called Minecraft, they're invited to create homes, build cities, or even craft a new universe—"if you can dream it, you can build it." They know the lure of ninjas and wizards and other magical creatures. They read books by the dozen and they play interactive games on screens that light up the night. Pretending comes naturally to them. They can play covert agents in the shape of imaginary box structures, build fantastical creatures that look like robots, and create mythical cities that rule the universe. Legos and Lincoln Logs hardly measure up. Imaginary characters roll off their tongues like creatures they've known all their lives. I cannot keep any of it straight. What is human and what is animal? Neither? What is true and what is imaginary? When I was a child we only knew fairy tales and cartoon characters that most often featured real or imagined people. This new world of role-playing games, of armed warriors and powerful wizards who battle one another and who build and destroy new and old worlds, is foreign to me. For them, mythology is real, even legendary; science fiction is their passion, all of it bigger than life and a part of their everyday lives.

This seemingly insatiable desire to pretend or make-believe seems to be timeless in spite of the fact that adolescence will soon have its way with them and then the dark ages will ensue for a few years. For me, a doting grandmother whose time with grandchildren is more cherished than words can describe, perhaps pretending and make-believe might be a sign of "second childhood." I hope so. The chance to become a child again somehow evokes in me silly seriousness that I welcome and they adore. We take our cues from one another. Absurdity and nonsense rule. Drama is the name of the game. The more, the better. And when finally we are sated with laughter, their holy faces shining and eyes sparkling, I am overcome with love and gratitude for these cherished children who grace our lives with such joy.

I am not captivated by the faceless features of the Minecraft characters and their ilk. But faces are another matter and I can pretend with the best of them. When in winter the soft gray-green moss hanging from the trees on our mountain becomes a delicious salad embellished by acorns and pine needles—the better to feed starving children—their faces light up. They can imagine nothing more delicious. Or those noisy birds overhead screeching their warnings—might they be spies or foreign agents guarding the forest? We take time to look at the cloud formations across the valley where layers of shrouded fog line the horizon to create new and ever-changing patterns and figures. They point out a sudden movement in the undergrowth where a tiny rabbit darts from one hole to another. We imagine that wild bundle of fur a beloved kitten or a frightening baby mountain lion. Has it been sent on an errand by its mother? Or was it encroaching on another's nest? Perhaps we should invite it for tea or moss salad? And look! Look here. It's a metal box with markings. "Geocaching!" they both exclaim, eyes wide. It's a way of spending time outside using technology skills and tools like GPS, Google, and the Geocaching app to find treasures in unlikely places. There are notes and small toys inside the box. Imagine!

Soon we make our way back up to the top of the hill. We must find our warm cottage and the bowls of porridge we know are ready for us and the waiting car is just the cottage we'd hoped for. Devouring our steaming porridge and drinking warm gulps of apple cider, the car cottage grows warm and its windows steam up. By now we all are drowsy with sleepiness and ready to find our real cottage. So the pretend cottage transforms into a vehicle and we make our way out of the car park for a short ride home. Soon it will be nighttime and then bedtime. "Can you tell us the rest of the story from last night?" they ask. "The one about the cabin and the beach and the sky in the middle of the night . . . the one where you pretended you were flying." Oh, the places we've been!

REFLECTION

Playing make-believe and "let's pretend" are short-lived moments in childhood. May the pleasure of their shining faces never be forgotten.

- When did you last play make-believe or "let's pretend"? Describe it.
- What about the magic of pretending is appealing to all ages?
- The playfulness of children is contagious. What stories or games do you enjoy sharing with children?
- Tell about an experience of make-believe or magic during your own childhood. What was it like?

23

Unseen faces

THERE IS SOME LATENT awareness of the faceless, the forgotten ones hidden in every society, but so often we go blithely about our business ignoring or forgetting the unseen. Not long ago, I was privileged to watch a documentary about the work of a French street artist known simply as JR.[1] A generous man whose deep humanity and open heart is apparent in every project, JR began in his own poor neighborhood in Paris using his skills as a photographer to capture the faces of unseen women, men, and children in what then were considered illicit graffiti posters. His larger-than-life exhibits, often posted surreptitiously, became a way of honoring them, of making them visible and acknowledging their humanity. The immediacy and "real-ness" of those oversized images—made of paper and glue from photographs—captured the attention of his country. JR then began sharing his people's art around the world. He went to the border between the United States and Mexico to photograph and create enormous public posters of the faces of children and their families struggling to cross the border to a safe and better way of life. Among those powerful pictures is a giant photograph of a child's face looking over a separation wall built in 2017 and a depiction of people eating together around a long

1. See the documentary *Paper & Glue* about JR's work.

table straddling both sides of the US-Mexican border. Holy faces around a holy table.

JR's unforgettably bold images of poor women living in favelas in South America, makeshift tenements hiding the faces of wrenching poverty and noble spirits, depict intelligent eyes and worn and tired expressions of pleasure at being recognized, known. His huge photographs posted across the dilapidated shelters covering an entire mountainside above the city of Rio de Janeiro reveal human beings too easily relegated to the margins of society, ignored and forgotten, their faces marked by unbelievable poverty and the daily grind of holding onto life. In similar ways, this artist portrays faces in a high security prison, first getting to know some of the inmates as he listens to the stories of their lives, their regrets and fears. His ability is deeply humanitarian, capturing the faces and the lives of individuals too easily forgotten and condemned, the holy faces of human beings created in the image of God no matter their status or lack of it. The street art of JR is audacious and bold as he travels the world recognizing and celebrating the beauty and dignity of unseen faces. And it's usually accompanied with personal involvement and interaction with the communities he photographs. Today his mesmeric photos are recognized in public spaces like the Brooklyn Museum and the Louvre pyramid.

Stories of unseen faces may be more common in this cable news era of 24-7 information. But honoring, recognizing, and truly *seeing* the unseen and forgotten is more than watching occasional humanitarian stories that appear on our screens, capturing our attention for a split second before we move on to other things. It is conscious willingness to do more than watch the news, to live with our eyes wide open, to feel with compassion and empathy, and to act on behalf of others. Seeing the unseen means getting outside our own spheres of comfort to experience the loneliness of the elderly, the isolation of poverty, the shame of a prison sentence, or the overwhelming confusion of being an immigrant. In our own self-absorption and preoccupation, it's easy to live without *really* seeing one another.

When a pandemic rears its ugly head, the reminder of the importance of faces becomes a daily experience. After COVID-19 went viral around the world and protection from masks came to be a critically important habit and necessary routine, isolation became even more trying as people struggled to recognize one another, their faces hidden behind masks—seeing without seeing. This searing experience has given us firsthand knowledge for understanding the importance of being seen, recognized, and acknowledged. But in my city and around the globe, there are many more unseen faces hidden among makeshift tents and shelters, in public housing and nursing homes, in prisons and institutions where mentally challenged people are housed, and in ghettos of the rich and ghettos where poverty is the order of the day—all spaces visible and invisible.

Where are the unseen faces in your world? After a long season of pandemic-induced isolation—a season exponentially more difficult for those living in poverty or incarceration or as refugees, how do *we* open our eyes and our hearts to one another? It feels like a new day in some ways—there's a certain euphoria about the freedom to really see one another again. Perhaps this opening of our eyes can be extended beyond the circles of the easily seen. How do *we* tend to the houseless, a lonely elderly neighbor, the young person sorting out identity issues and too afraid to come out? How shall *we* see the faces of those hidden away in institutions or in their own homes? There are so many barriers to being seen and recognized, so many walls behind which to disappear. How shall *we* deal with the default of "out of sight, out of mind?"

Let us resist the temptation to categorize or demonize or refuse to see one another. May we live with the openhearted empathy, honesty, and unconditional mercy and love that motivate a passionate artist like JR as he showcases so many unseen faces. Help us learn to live with humility and unease about our own comfort and security, recognizing our own vulnerability and insecurity. May compassion and empathy allow us to see with eyes wide open the hidden places where the unseen faces of fellow human beings sometimes disappear. Every face is holy.

REFLECTION

Unseen faces are legion. May we open our eyes to all who too easily slip out of sight and out of mind. Every face is holy.

- Where are the unseen faces in your world?
- Name some literal ways for recognizing and interacting with those outside our own circles of the easily seen.
- Describe what it means to you that every face is holy.

24

Unspeakable joy!

Perhaps you, dear reader, have had the experience of being completely and unequivocally caught off guard? Something entirely off your screen or an experience you never saw coming or some other surprise has left you unexpectedly speechless, even amazed or dumbfounded. When it happens that this is dreaded news or an unhappy surprise, the turn life may take stops us in our tracks as we numbly assess the situation. But when the news is joyful? Watch out, world! We've all endured a very long season of discouragement and so much bad news—the anguish and fear of a worldwide pandemic, political chaos beyond our wildest imaginings, ongoing racial injustice and gun violence, war. One of these tragedies would be enough to send us reeling. All of them together are wrenching. The particular joy that came to us not so many months ago was unbridled and unexpected, a long overdue experience of genuine, unspeakable joy.

Our daughter phoned one day with a rather nonchalant invitation to stop by in the afternoon when she and her family would all be at home. We were leaving on a trip in a day or two and they wanted to say good-bye. Her rather ordinary invitation that momentous afternoon was not unusual and so when the time came and we knew our little grandsons (then seven and nine) would be home from school, we wrapped up a warm loaf of banana bread for the boys and arrived soon after. We might have picked up on the signals had we had any inkling about what to expect but we were clueless. They all four sat down beside each other as we came into their home, the younger brother alternating laser-focused stares toward his mother and father, the dog bouncing recklessly from person to person. Questions were asked about our pending trip and we recalled traveling with the boys when they were younger, remembering how we practiced speaking to the flight attendants and re-imagining the wonders of flying.

Kai, pensive and earnest, was quiet and seemed uncomfortably distracted. Kieran, *always* ready for adventure, kept looking at his mother, waiting impatiently for the small talk to end. When he could wait no longer, his mother and father, their eyes shining, told us they had something important to share. In the hushed moment that followed with both boys' faces riveted on their parents, our youngest daughter and son-in-law announced their joy over the coming of a new baby. Not just any baby but another newborn in our family, another miracle, another brand-new life! And though we are seasoned grandparents who understand how babies are created and who are more than fond of this role of grandparenting, we had no clue and the joy of such an unexpected surprise left us speechless and awestruck. It was as if time had stopped and the world had shifted. I'd not felt such unspeakable joy in a very long time.

The brothers who'd been told this momentous news prior to our arrival had polar-opposite reactions. Kieran, no shrinking violet who chafes over being the youngest family member, was overjoyed and could hardly contain his excitement. His serious older brother, Kai, had burst into uncontrollable sobs, overcome by so unexpected a change in their lives. "*You* caused this, Kieran! It's all *your* fault—*you* made this happen," he proclaimed through tears, looking for someone to blame. "You're the one who wanted a baby!" And in the next weeks and months as we all adjusted, we watched our daughter's slowly-growing "baby bump," our thoughts consumed by this little one still in utero, still hidden from us. Who will "it" be? What name will this beloved child have? What stages of development are happening this month?

The beautifully descriptive words of the psalmist, "For you created my inmost being, you knit me together in my mother's womb" (Ps 139:13) echo across time. The profound miracle of a new human being seems anything but ordinary or mundane. And despite the fact that we all come into this world in the same way, we know the risks, the complete absence of joy in the darkness and pain of unwanted pregnancy, the many horrific and anguishing circumstances that are far from joyful or celebrative. For many who wish to have children and can't, it may be agonizing to hear another's joy over the promise of a child. Life is not fair. But when a child is wanted and longed for, the joy is dramatic, contagious. Names began to be tossed about, the brothers choosing their favorites, the parents holding their ideas close, unwilling to have them critiqued or commented on by too-willing family members and friends or to settle too quickly without knowing this new little one. Now we wait to discover this child's holy face, to know its gender, to count fingers and toes, whether it will have curly hair like its brothers, eye color, temperament, and yes, the name. So much mystery! This child who is being knitted together week after week in its mother's womb is both hidden and present, known and unknown. With the psalmist, our voices join in affirmation, "I praise you because I am fearfully and wonderfully made; your works are wonderful, I know that full well" (Ps 139:14).

We do know this full well. Every new life comes with a holy face. The gift of life is indeed a miracle, incomprehensible, mysterious. We are filled with gratitude when good health prevails, when regular doctor's reports and scans show a baby who is growing and thriving, when a healthy child finally is born. We are grateful for strong and wise mothers, for equally supportive and wise fathers, both engaged and present. We give thanks for siblings and grandparents and family and friends who share their own joy, affirming the goodness of life and welcoming a new child with overwhelming love and support. We also do not forget the pain and heartbreak of so many who find themselves in a dark place, not ready or able to care for a child, or for whom birth will be life-threatening or for whom pregnancy is no gift. But for us now, unspeakable joy is the order of the day and a gift like no other. Watch out, world! We wait with exuberant expectation for this treasured new life, this holy face, this child about to be born.

REFLECTION

Every new life comes with a holy face. This particular new life for us, now, is unspeakable joy!

- When the promise of new life is an affirmation of love and the goodness of life, we are overjoyed. When that isn't the case, it's quite a different story. I hope readers will indulge the joy shared here and perhaps share their own stories, some of which may not be joyful.
- Words seem inadequate when there is joy and gratitude over the gift of life. Describe a time when you shared a birth. What was it like?
- Our culture struggles with many issues surrounding pregnancy and birth. Pro-life and pro-choice positions hardly describe the complexities. When pregnancy is not a gift, then what?
- When have you felt unspeakable joy?

25

Where God Shows Up

My life has been steeped in God talk. And yet, *and yet*, I am one who grapples most days to make sense of religion and the world, to understand the holy, to make sense of God. I often find questions more interesting than answers and nuance more beautiful than precise statements or pat definitions. I am comfortable with doubt and lack of certitude. For me, God does not necessarily show up in paintings or icons, and doctrines and symbols too are only partial interpretations. My childish notions of a God somewhere distant, a physical being, a kind shepherd, or a powerful monarch, a face, failed me long ago. God shows up most often for me in others, in glimpses of goodwill or sacrifice, in reverence and respect and humility. With Jewish Rabbi Abraham Joshua Heschel, I have learned to imagine God resting on our eyelids, present in every moment of life and death and beyond. In conversations with Muslim acquaintances and in the common ground we share with Jewish friends, our concepts of God are expanded further. Our mutual quest to know God or perhaps more accurately, to be known *by* God, is life-giving and lifelong.

Holy faces are where I see God. In a circle of friends gathered together around the lighting of a candle, God shows up in the tenderness and mercy of authentic conversation and shared vulnerability. God is present in the throes of depression or addiction or other illnesses, weeping with and for such suffering—often in the faces of caregivers and loving communities who make more of us and more of the world, who help make us whole. In nature and the changing patterns of the seasons, we also see the face of the sacred. In the birth of a child, a mystery we barely comprehend and a gift like no other, God shows up making co-creators of us and telling us *we* are made in God's image. We belong to a long line of searchers seeking the face of God, longing to understand ourselves and the complicated world we share. Where do you see the holy one who inhabits each of us and all of creation, showing us how to love the world and ourselves?

Brian Doyle was an extraordinary writer and observer whose presence in life and now in death continues to show us a life *steeped* in the goodness of God. Faithful Catholic that he was, he understood symbols and rituals and the myriad ways they convey the holy. But by some extraordinary gift of sight and imagination, of mindfulness, Doyle saw God in all of creation. In and among his long sentences, his meandering thoughts, his attention to detail, Brian Doyle captured the presence of the holy in birds and bears, in rivers and on mountains, in esteem for things animate and inanimate, in his tender love for his children and his family, in the pleasure he found from relationships with others. Without a lot of God talk, he leaves no doubt in his stunning writing about the presence of God. His reverence for nature is itself holy. His passionate love of life and of humanity is authentic, genuine. God shows up in the life and work of Brian Doyle. In mountains that speak and martens that communicate with humans, in the life of a crow named Moses and a village by the sea.

Many of us are overwhelmed by an unrelenting stream of communication from ubiquitous cell phones connecting us to one another in ways we couldn't have imagined a few years ago. The *too much* of instant communication—whether phone calls, texts, emails, photos, or on social media—is both bane and blessing. It has the capacity to numb us in our frantic efforts to keep up and it requires discipline. But there is this: our ability to maintain and nurture truly significant relationships, to relate with and care for others has increased exponentially. Whether long exchanges or short with people we care about in every corner of the world, with acquaintances and everyone else with whom we wish to relate, this ability to connect is another of the places where God shows up. We all know what it is to be lonely or isolated; to endure illness or worry or hardship of one kind or another; we are part of a vast web of connections, connected with all of creation, and we need each other's holy faces. For all the downsides of instant communication (and they are legion), the ability and privilege of relationships and connections are places where God shows up. I say this with passion because the truth of it is stunning.

Talking this week with family living in South Africa reminds me how close they actually are—with one click we hear their voices and look into each other's faces. Texts and phone calls relay concern for a grandchild hospitalized with pneumonia. With that one click, she (from her hospital bed) and I (in another hemisphere) talk about our last visit where we imagined ourselves lost in a forest—laughing over make-believe and our silly play. A visit with a dear friend living now in a retirement home far from where I live reminds me of the joy and pleasure she is, of her wit and humor, of the many meals we've shared and the conversations we've savored. Two cousins, both artists, regularly share themselves by posting striking pictures of beautiful gardens and lovely paintings; former colleagues keep me connected to their lives, their work, their corners of the world. For me these are glimpses of God, holy faces, places where God shows up to illustrate the goodness of life.

God showed up throughout the trauma of my brother's death. In the holy faces of our grieving family and others who came to comfort us, there was a palpable sense of the holy one, the spirit of a loving God grieving with and for us. And I wonder if God didn't speak to us as well in the eerie presence of two eagles perched for more than an hour that afternoon in the trees above the beach where we gathered and in the dragonflies that careened around the park where we said our farewells.

Today in a series of exchanges with a wise and wide circle of friends and family, my spouse and I feel their nearness even from long distances. We're grateful for deer grazing outside our windows, keenly aware of the privilege of life together, of constancy and faithfulness. We saw the sun rise this morning over a mountain to the east, coming a bit earlier every day as we approach the summer solstice. Those rays of light and warmth are surely places where God shows up. And walking last evening along a river where green glacial waters surge through the mountains that surround us reminds me of the goodness of creation, of clean water and air, of breathtaking beauty and the joy of this season. Even in the cycle of seasons, of rain and snow and worry over all the signs of global warming, there is something of the wonder and mystery of a God who creates new life, restores, and renews.

In my tradition, the Eucharist is shared each Sunday, bread and wine around a table where God's presence is so tangible as to be unnerving. The table is as wide as the welcome, *the body of Christ, broken for you, the blood of Christ, poured out for you* said over and over again as if the one receiving and the one serving are the only ones in the room. They know this to be a holy act: life-giving bread and drink poured out for a broken world and our own broken lives. Every Sunday is a little Easter, a reminder of new life and resurrection, of fresh beginnings and new starts, reminding each of us that *we* are Christ's body, the food needed to sustain and nourish a hurting world. Whether helping serve or being served this simple meal, I look into other faces, other eyes as together we receive bread that is more than bread, wine that is more than drink. God shows up in every encounter where we become bread and drink for another. We become what we receive, the very body of Christ. If you've ever served a meal at a homeless shelter or invited strangers to your own table or visited someone in a treatment center or in prison, if you've ever shared bottles of water or cups of coffee with someone who is thirsty, or been the recipient of such acts, be aware! God is there—in the bread and wine, in your own holy face, and in the holy faces of those you serve.

Holy faces are where I see God. Where does the presence or the mystery of the sacred, of God, show up for you? When or where are you aware of someone, something beyond or within the realities of your own life, a holy presence, a holy face? Where God shows up might be indefinable or confusing while also providing you the comfort of identity, familiarity, and belonging. Whether you are part of a faith community or not, a devout Muslim, Christian, or practicing Jew, a Buddhist, an atheist, or any other manifestation of belief, may the God who rests on our eyelids help us see the places where God shows up. Perhaps this reflection will serve as a gateway into circles of conversation outside our own traditions, our own beliefs. That in itself might underscore our common humanity and our common longing to make sense of our lives and our place in this world. Oh, the places where God shows up!

REFLECTION

May the God who rests on our eyelids reveal to us the inscrutable holy one who inhabits all of creation.

- Where do you see the holy one showing us how to love the world and ourselves?
- Describe some of the holy faces in your life.
- How do you honor other ways of knowing God, respecting other cultures and traditions?

26

Wise women

The holy faces of wise women and the circles of conversation we share have been a constant in my life. They have brought depth and substance—richness—in ways too numerous to count. Whether face to face, often in circles of one kind or another, or in spaces made sacred by the depth of friendship and trust, over cups of tea and at long distances, I am grateful beyond words for their presence and camaraderie. From lifelong relationships with sisters, to friends both old and new, near and far, to acquaintances who became colleagues and mentors, the grace and love of wise women continue to hallow my daily life. Gender is part of it but often it's mostly about *presence*—simple and not so simple *presence*—the extraordinary ability to be open to and with one another, vulnerable and willing to engage in life together. Together our lives are mutually enlivened and enriched.

These exemplary individuals who happen to be women fit first into **personal relationships**. They are women with whom I've gathered over many years to share joy and sorrow, stages of life, challenges and affirmations, curiosity and a love of learning. Their willingness to journey together is generous and engaging, an investment of immeasurable consequence. From them I have learned kindness and mutuality. From them I have learned resilience and accountability. From them I have learned to make more of the world and more of myself. They are the women in my life who give themselves away, helping others to live more meaningfully, who have a sense of humor and who see and make beauty while paying attention to the state of the world and its deepest needs. They know the meaning of unconditional love and grace. They are mothers and daughters and sisters, women with noteworthy professional lives, spouses and caregivers, friends from university days and neighbors from around the world, teachers and professors and colleagues who model the best of what it means to be human, religious leaders and clergy, all from whom I have learned so much—so many holy faces. To be gifted with wise women throughout one's life is empowering.

Wise women in my life also fall into a second category I call **women of extraordinary influence**. Just as personal relationships expand across a lifetime, so too with influential individuals. These are women whose exemplary humanity and impact on the lives of others is life-changing, names readers might recognize. Their lives are worthy of emulation. Holy heroes like Sweden's Greta Thunberg and Pakistan's Malala Yousafzai, both of them activists who from very young ages have enlightened the world with their commitments to climate change and the rights of women. Their single-mindedness has cost them dearly but they are unrelenting in their pursuits of a safer and more just planet. Both have become faces for change around the world. Malala Yousafzai won the Nobel Peace Prize at the age of seventeen; Thunberg was *Time Magazine*'s youngest Person of the Year (2019) and has been nominated for the Nobel multiple times. American lawyer and jurist, Ruth Bader Ginsburg, was a presence and voice to be reckoned with on the Supreme Court in the United States and indefatigable as she helped pave the way for equal rights for women. American poet Amanda Gorman uses her gifts to write pithy, rhythmic verses about race and gender, power and corruption, hope and honesty. Former Speaker of the House Nancy Pelosi has been unrelenting in her life's work on behalf of children and families. She led her colleagues in Congress with dignity, persevering against enormous resistance. Prominent Russian human rights activist Anna Politkovskaya lost her life several years ago because of commitments to fact-finding and truth in a country where neither seem to matter.

Other public servants who model the importance of human rights and democratic values include American feminist and abortion rights activist Cecile Richards; journalists like Maria Ressa, another Nobel Prize winner who continues to fight for freedom of expression in the Philippines by revealing the abuses of authoritarianism; American historian and political analyst Heather Cox Richardson, whose "Letters from an American" appear in a nightly newsletter with over a million readers; and Rachel Maddow, whose work in broadcasting and writing focuses on current and past political crises. These wise women and so many, many more are committed to accountability and the common good as they demand integrity and truth-telling in government and beyond. Their lives of service and selflessness embody qualities that make more of our world and more of us. With millions of others, I regularly gather around "their tables" seeking out the wisdom of their company.

And because reading and writing are central to my life, I highlight a few powerfully influential **women writers** whose books inspire and challenge. The circles of conversations described above very often focus on books and their female authors. In my childhood home a lot of years ago, I learned to love books from the moment I could read. As is always the case with reading, whole new worlds were opened and the look and feel of books and words and their ability to transform and inspire continue to captivate me. The neighborhood library was holy ground and the world of books has introduced me to hundreds of wise women who are central in my life. One of these is writer Marilynne Robinson, whose ability to develop a few unforgettable characters is matched by the ways she illustrates human relationships, the complexities of religion, and small town living. Another is Barbara Brown Taylor, who has given me words and images for expanding our often narrow views of religion and daily life, and Sara Miles, who writes eloquently about what it means to feed people and the role religion plays in helping her discover this. From writers like Toni Morrison, Maya Angelou, and Isabell Wilkerson, my eyes continue to be opened by the plague of racism and classism undermining all our lives and calling for radical justice and change.

From authors as disparate as Virginia Woolf, Barbara Kingsolver, Louise Erdrich, and Willa Cather, I've learned the importance of female voices and female groundbreaking. From Michelle Obama's life and writing, I continue to uncover the power of tenacity and transparency from her uniquely feminine perspective. She too highlights the significance of wise women and their circles of female conversation around the tables of all our lives. The women in Elena Ferrante's series about Neapolitan life in mid-twentieth-century Naples is a powerful exhibit of female friendship. I admire contemporary writers like Anne Lamott, Ann Patchett, and Anna Quindlen. Even this small sampling of writers has made a profoundly powerful impact on the lives of women. To my mind, learning from authentic conversation with wise women in personal relationships, from exemplary individuals who happen to be women, and from the world of remarkable women writers helps define a meaningful life.

And where do these exchanges with wise women take place? Always in the ordinary rhythms of everyday life—on the evening news, in daily posts, often around tables and other welcoming circles of hospitality and openness, in the quiet of a reading corner. Sometimes in the darkness of suffering where shared pain is common ground, where we all experience humility and grace. Always where there is joy to be celebrated, achievements to mark, or reasons for a party. Sometimes just by happenstance when we realize that life is better shared and we aren't meant to "go it alone." Often when we're afraid or insecure or when worry stalks us undermining our sense of self, our agency and our power.

All of us know ordinary individuals—friends and neighbors, acquaintances—who walk regularly and intentionally with people whose lives are difficult for one reason or another. The young woman who spends her days with cancer patients helping them manage treatments they hope will extend their lives; a couple (their numbers are legion) who deliver pots of soup or loaves of bread to anyone needing food or a bit of comfort; foster parents, chaplains, medical professionals, and social workers; female jurists and legal experts who help immigrants find their way in a new land or seek justice when injustice seems the default; generous neighbors who drop everything to surround a grieving family; teachers who care for their students beyond the classroom. I include my friend who fosters aging or sick animals at every turn and another whose life is focused on daily connections of compassion, showing empathy I sometimes envy. All of these holy faces are ordinary human beings whose generosity of spirit and willingness to make the world a better place transforms lives, human and otherwise.

So gather around the tables of your life! Invite women you consider to be wise, interesting, and empathetic. Listen to the voices of women making radical changes in a world that needs their honest and courageous perspective. Notice friends and neighbors who do the daily tasks of making the world a better place. Surround yourself with holy faces. Create circles of conversation. Seek out women who have learned to be present, single-handedly making a difference whether in family life, care for their neighbors, human rights, or racial equity. Finally, read women writers whose books inspire and inform, comfort and challenge. The holy faces of wise women make the world a better place.

REFLECTION

Embrace the gift of being empowered by wise women. Seek out the company of women who challenge and inspire and who make the world a better place.

- Name a few of the wise women in your life. What characteristics attract you to them?
- What is it about gender-based groups that makes them unique? That limits them?
- Describe circles of conversation you've found worthwhile. Are they topical? Do they center around a common interest, a common need? What makes them worthwhile?
- Women writers! Who are your favorites? What makes reading them so important for you?

Bibliography

Durka, Gloria. *Praying with Julian of Norwich.* Winona, MN: Saint Mary's University of Minnesota Press, 1989.

The Emmy Awards. "Fred Rogers Acceptance Speech—1997." *YouTube*, March 26, 2008. https://www.youtube.com/watch?v=Upm9LnuCBUM&t=1s.

Erdrich, Louise. *The Painted Drum.* New York: HarperCollins, 2005.

The Grouped Churches of St St Colman's, Kilroot and St John's, Ballycarry. "Asked by the BBC . . ." *Facebook*, May 1, 2021. https://www.facebook.com/100600784923231/photos/a.101619388154704/311926510457323/?locale=pt_BR.

Hoster, Elizabeth Merrill. "The Man Who Contained . . ." *Facebook*, December 26, 2021. https://www.facebook.com/photo/?fbid=10159850340926948&set=a.10151046468451948.

Human Library. "About the Human Library." https://humanlibrary.org/about/.

JR. *Paper & Glue.* Beverly Hills, CA: Imagine Documentaries, 2021.

Julian of Norwich. *Julian of Norwich's Showings.* Translated by Edmund Colledge and James Walsh. Classics of Western Spirituality. New York: Paulist, 1978.

Lewis, John. *Across That Bridge: A Vision for Change and the Future of America.* New York: Hyperion, 2012.

Luciano Pavarotti. "Eric Clapton, Luciano Pavarotti, East London Gospel Choir —Holy Mother (Live)." *YouTube*, May 10, 2019. https://www.youtube.com/watch?v=x9uYu4R2nk8.

Mayntz, Melissa. "35 Fun Facts about Hummingbirds." *The Spruce* (blog), March 24, 2023. https://www.thespruce.com/fun-facts-about-hummingbirds-387106.

Oliver, Mary. "Why I Wake Early." In *Devotions*, 171. New York: Penguin, 2017.

———. "The Buddha's Last Instruction." In *House of Light*, 4–5. Boston: Beacon, 1990.

Palmer, Parker J. "In Times of Deep Darkness." *Facebook*, December 9, 2019. https://www.facebook.com/parkerjpalmer/photos/a.448150067077/10156801875812078/.

———. "My Heart Is Broken . . ." *Facebook*, March 11, 2020. https://www.facebook.com/parkerjpalmer/.

Pennington, M. Basil. *Listening: God's Word for Today*. New York: Continuum, 2000.

Pinkstone, Joe. "Hummingbirds Can Drop Their Body Temperature below 40°F When They Rest to Save Energy for the Next Day." *Daily Mail*, September 9, 2020. https://www.dailymail.co.uk/sciencetech/article-8713499/Hummingbirds-lower-body-temperature-4-C-night.html.

Skinner, John, ed. *Revelation of Love*. New York: Doubleday, 1997.

Tutu, Desmond. *No Future without Forgiveness*. New York: Doubleday, 1999.

Tutu, Desmond, and Mpho Tutu. *The Book of Forgiving*. New York: HarperOne, 2014.

———. *Made for Goodness*. San Francisco: HarperOne, 2011.

"12 Most Interesting Facts about Hummingbirds." We Love Hummingbirds (blog), n.d. https://www.welovehummingbirds.com/blogs/news/interesting-facts-about-hummingbirds.

Vanover, Lori. "Hummingbird Size: How Much Does a Hummingbird Weigh?" *Birds & Blooms* (blog), March 15, 2022. https://www.birdsandblooms.com/birding/attracting-hummingbirds/how-much-does-hummingbird-weigh/.

Weinmann, Katharine. "I Sometimes Forget." *A Wabi Sabi Life* (blog), October 29, 2021. https://awabisabilife.ca/2021/10/29/i-sometimes-forget/.

Wilde, Katelyn. "Do Hummingbirds Have Feet?" Sonoma Birding (blog), n.d. https://www.sonomabirding.com/do-hummingbirds-have-feet/.

Williamson, Sheri L. *Hummingbirds of North America*. Boston: Houghton Mifflin, 2001.

Made in United States
Troutdale, OR
12/26/2023

16411551R00090